To Kathy.

Thanks for being such an ambassador of Analytical Reading.

Michael

Giving the Sense

How to Read Aloud With Meaning

Nedra Newkirk Lamar
and the
Institute of Analytical Reading

Including material from
How to Speak the Written Word
by
Nedra Newkirk Lamar

INSTITUTE OF

ANALYTICAL READING
INCORPORATED

Printed in the United States of America

Library of Congress control number: 2016937199

ISBN 978-1-945170-24-9

FIRST EDITION

CONSULTANTS CLEARING HOUSE
PUBLISHER

So they read in the book in the law of God distinctly,
and gave the sense,
and caused them to understand the reading.

NEHEMIAH 8:8

Contents

PREFACE

About This Handbook

Early in her professional life, Nedra Newkirk Lamar, the inspiration for this handbook, was asked to judge a speaking contest. One of the contest rules was that the contestants were not to memorize their presentation but simply to speak from their knowledge of the assigned subject. Others may have been fooled, but Lamar could tell that some speakers had memorized their talk, and she knew the exact sections they had scripted.

Nedra Lamar, a student of Latin and Greek who also trained for the theater, a teacher in expression, and a pioneer in the American standard of diction, had observed that "everything we say or read or write is just a procession of little grammatical constructions, and without realizing it we phrase and emphasize each one in the same way every time we use it." Lamar could tell that those contestants who had memorized their talk did not follow these natural patterns. They were not speaking conversationally, but were saying words they had written down and memorized.

As she coached actors and speakers and listened to others talking conversationally, she discovered and identified basic principles of phrasing and emphasis. Some of these principles had been known to educators in these fields for years. The principle of emphasizing new and subduing old ideas, for example, had been found even in books teaching English to the non-English speaker. But she began to see more speech patterns, such as how we connect ideas that logically belong together and separate ideas that don't belong together. To her knowledge, these principles and patterns had never been set down together in any kind of systematic order for people to apply.

Her classes in the new "American" standard of diction (as opposed to the "Continental" standard) were so popular that some people kept coming for the second and third years. The fourth year she decided she should have an advanced class for the fourth-year people, a class in reading aloud conversationally, although she had never heard of such a thing previously.

This class was to change the direction of her work. At first Lamar thought she would teach actors to read lines as if they were just talking, but the demand for her coaching expanded to helping public speakers and readers of published works, including the Bible. In 1949 she wrote out these principles of conversational reading in her book, *How to Speak the Written Word; A Guide to Effective Public Reading*. It was the first to identify conversational patterns and has remained a leader in this subject even today. The book has been purchased every year since 1949 by students who read the written word aloud, and has been reprinted multiple times to meet this demand.

No subject is static, and as Lamar continued to discover new patterns of conversational speech, she identified how these principles could be applied to reading aloud. She revised *How to Speak the Written Word* in 1967. Later she published new principles in papers for her students, the most significant of which is her discovery of a principle of emphasis she came to call "Common Denominator."

By 1967, Lamar's private student load had increased to the point where she had to train others to teach from her text. In 1973 she formed the Institute of Analytical Reading to further the teaching of the principles of reading aloud and to ensure that her high ethical standard of teaching would be maintained.

Which brings us to the reason for this handbook. After 67 years since the publication of *How to Speak the Written Word* and 49 years since the last revision, and many years more of discovery and teaching, it is time to pull together all the work of Nedra Newkirk Lamar into one new updated and easy to read handbook.

The title, *Giving the Sense* was how Lamar described the value of her system of reading aloud. She wanted her students to read the authors' words using the principles and conversational patterns that bring out the ideas the authors were conscious of as they were writing. The listeners then would get the sense the author intended and not a personal interpretation—or misrepresentation—of the reader.

In the following pages, whenever you see personal pronouns indicating first person voice, you are reading Lamar's own words.

PART ONE

Getting Started

1

What is Analytical Reading?

If someone asked you, "What are the essentials of good oral reading?" would you say, "A good reader must have a beautiful voice. He or she must read with great conviction, and must never make a mistake?" Though these characteristics may be admirable, I feel that you could have them all and still lack the essentials. What might be missing from such reading? **The meaning.**

In my opinion, there are three indispensable requirements for good reading:

1. Audible voice. After all, why bring out the meaning if no one behind the fifth row can hear you?

2. Intelligible diction. What's the good of being heard, if your listeners can't figure out the words?

3. **The meaning. The MEANING!** What's the point of a reading if your audience doesn't understand the ideas behind the words?

Whose meaning? The writer's. Not what the reader wishes the writer had meant. Not what the writer **did** mean somewhere **else**, but what the writer means **right here**.

So how do we determine the meaning? Imagine the writer is speaking to you. Because of his or her inflection, emphasis and phrasing you naturally understand the meaning. That's because of the common patterns and principles of conversational speech that indicate the ideas the words are intended to convey. Once the writer sets these words to paper (or to a computer), these patterns and principles now exist in the writing but need to be discovered by the reader.

You may not be conscious of these principles and patterns today, but once you begin to recognize them, you will see them embedded in the text. You will then read ideas instead of words. You will hear the writer speaking.

We call the study and application of these conversational patterns, and principles based on logic and simple grammar, Analytical Reading. By applying these principles to the material you are reading, you will discover the ideas—the meaning—presented by the writer. Many people, who have no intention of ever reading before an audience, congregation, or microphone, study Analytical Reading in order to see for themselves the meaning of deeply philosophical writings. An editor who did such a study told me, "A page of print will never look the same to me again. Now I see ideas, not just words."

Once the meaning is clear to you, the reader, the principles of Analytical Reading will show you how to make this clear to your audience. Analytical Reading draws the hearer's attention from the reader and his style to the writer and to what the writer is saying.

In this book you will learn how to ask yourself simple questions, such as, "What is the new idea here?" or "Is the writer implying a contrast?" "Is this phrase connected with the one that comes before or after it?" The analysis is not complicated or onerous; it does not require a PhD. As you master these principles, you will find that even complex passages will unravel and you can read them intelligently and naturally. You will see meanings that you have never noticed before and will be able to bring them out for your listeners.

2

Bringing Out the Meaning to Others

If you're going to serve your guests a cake, do you set before them a silver tray holding butter, sugar, flour, baking powder, milk, eggs, and vanilla? Most desirable ingredients, but who wants to eat ingredients? You must process them. All that your guests should have to do is eat the cake.

Too often oral readers give their hearers only the ingredients—the words. But the words need to be processed, and the three main ways of processing them are: **emphasis, phrasing**, and **inflection**.

In reading aloud, you are merely trying to reproduce the way you would say the same words in spontaneous conversation. You are trying to "be natural." But to be natural deliberately is not that easy. Haven't you known persons who, when placed before a camera and told to "look natural," immediately look unnatural and strained? They become self-conscious and can't remember how they look and feel when they look natural. Just so, an inexperienced reader, placed before an audience or a microphone and told to **read** naturally, has no idea how he would say the same words if he were just speaking them as they came to his thought.

The examples provided in this book include provable logical principles that show you the meaning, and conversational patterns that show you how to read so as to bring out the meaning in a natural way, as if you were just the writer talking.

Done well, the art and science of oral reading (just as in any presentation) requires the application of technique. Unless a violinist is one of those rare geniuses, she must have learned her notes, she must have perfected her technique, and then applied this knowledge and skill to the music before being able to play it well. The best compliment anyone can give the reader as well as the musician runs something like this: "You make it sound so easy."

The intention of Analytical Reading is not to influence the reader's interpretation, but to pose questions—to be answered by whom? By the reader himself in the light of logical principles, so that he sees possibilities he might otherwise have missed.

A characteristic of the readers who have applied these principles is that they do not speak or read alike. Their reading is not uniform or stereotyped. Four great pianists will play the same concerto so distinctively that a musician can tell one from the other; yet each pianist will be following the principles of the science of music, principles as firm as those of mathematics.

Four deft cooks will follow the same recipe for a cake and turn out different but delicious cakes. And yet the directions given in a cook book frequently are rigid, while the ideas set forth in this book are not. So don't be afraid that you will be copying someone else or reading like every other student of this book as you apply these principles. Instead of stifling individuality, spontaneity, and inspiration, Analytical Reading serves to increase them.

3

The Tools of Giving the Sense

The purpose of this book is to help you read naturally. The first essential for a reader of the written word, is to have a thorough understanding of the text. If he enjoys it, this is still better. But above all, he must understand it. The second requirement is equally important: to have the knowledge of how to express the meaning that he understands. This involves knowledge of where to pause and where not to pause, what to emphasize and what to subdue, and other points that will be discussed in this book.

How do we emphasize?

We most often emphasize a word by raising the pitch of our voice when we speak that word—in other words, we speak the accented syllable on a higher key of the musical scale than we use on the rest of the sentence. We do this unconsciously in everyday conversation.

Think of your normal voice pitch as your "Middle C" and the words that you emphasize (or stress if you prefer) spoken a note or two above your "Middle C". The broader the range in pitch, the greater the emphasis.

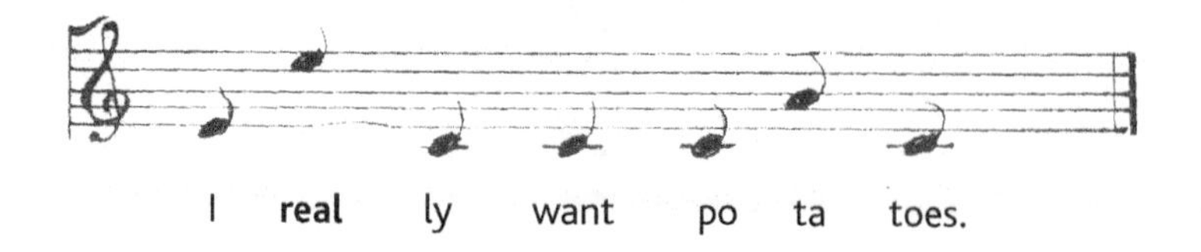

The counterpoint to emphasis, that of subduing a word or string of words, is achieved by keeping the pitch of your voice low when you speak that word or string of words. This seems to be difficult for some people. It may feel unnatural, especially subduing a string of words, yet we do it all the time in normal conversation. It is every bit as important in bringing out the meaning as emphasizing.

Less common ways of emphasizing

Other ways to emphasize include inserting pauses, slowing down, or changing the volume. Emphasis achieved by a pause before a word signals something new is about to come. A pause after the word may imply what you just heard was a new idea.

When you wish to give importance to a whole passage rather than merely to one word, you can change your tempo by slowing the rate of speed. This arrests the attention of listeners and concentrates their thought on that passage. Change in volume can be used as a means of emphasizing. Getting louder or getting softer when you speak the word you want to emphasize also catches the listener's attention.

To sum up, here is what we commonly do when we want to emphasize a word or words:

- **Most frequently**—Raise the pitch on the accented syllable
- Pause before or after the word

- Change the tempo of reading
- Change the volume

What is inflection?

Inflection is a bending of the voice. There are four kinds of inflection: level, rising, falling and circumflex.

A level inflection is not truly an inflection as the voice doesn't bend, but remains on the same pitch. A rising inflection is one in which the voice begins a syllable on one musical tone and then rises to a higher one. Rising inflections are used to denote uncertainty, a questioning attitude, and lack of finality.

A falling inflection is one in which the voice begins a syllable on one musical note and then falls to a lower one. Falling inflections denote finality or a statement, not a question.

When she comes back, we will finish the rehearsal.

In this example, you would use a rising inflection at the end of the first phrase, on the word *back,* and a falling inflection at the end of the sentence, on the final syllable *sal,* in the word *rehearsal.*

A circumflex inflection means by derivation a "bending around" and is achieved with a rising-falling, or falling-rising pitch within the vowel. Here from Psalm 18:30, is a circumflex on *God*, rising, falling and rising, all on one syllable:

As for God~, His way is perfect.

We discuss inflection in greater detail in Chapter 39. In the examples used throughout the handbook we will occasionally indicate where a certain inflection would sound more natural.

What is phrasing?

Phrasing is connecting ideas together that logically belong together by not pausing between them; and separating ideas that logically do not belong together by inserting a pause.

Emphasis and phrasing come in pairs. When you emphasize a word, there is usually another word or string of words you de-emphasize, or subdue. When you connect a phrase with a second phrase, you often disconnect it from another phrase.

Unless we have had training or practice we may not realize how timidly we are using these pairs when reading for others. Try this experiment: Without looking at a mirror, smile as if you are giving a presentation to an audience. Then hold that smile and turn to the mirror and see if it looks as naturally happy as you thought. If you are like most folks, probably not. Next make a really off-the-wall smile you think would look silly and then check it out in the mirror. Probably that's the face you **thought** you were presenting in the first instance. You will want to be just as definite in the use of your voice when you pause or vary your pitch.

This isn't about words. It's about ideas.

If we are speaking for the writer, we would want to use as much expression as the writer, but not more. This isn't about a performance by us, the reader. We only want the ideas we emphasize to stand out, the pauses we make to last long enough to be heard.

Conventions used in this book

In the following chapters we will be discussing certain words that appear in the sample illustrations. Whenever we discuss such a word you will find it *italicized* as in the following statement:

In the second example given earlier, you would emphasize *really* at a slightly higher pitch.

When we want to show the emphasis you might use in a passage, the emphasized or stressed word or words will be in **boldface**. Occasionally we will also use bold-face in our text to give more clarity to a point we are making. However, if you choose to mark the text you are going to read, you may find that underlining the words you want to emphasize will help your delivery.

How we mark emphasis:	I want **potatoes**
How you might mark emphasis:	I want potatoes

When we want to suggest places to pause for logical phasing, we will use a vertical bar | for a regular pause and two vertical bars || for an extended pause. For reasons we will explain in Chapter 12, we do not recommend inserting commas to indicate a pause.

Where a principle indicates no pause between two words, we will insert an underline between the two words as in.

I want potatoes_that are crispy

You might want to mark a connection by drawing a curved line across the bottom of the space between the words, reminding you to pass through the text without pausing.

Use of the Bible for examples

The Bible, in addition to being the most widely quoted book in the world, offers excellent opportunities to illustrate the principles of Analytical Reading. Unless otherwise noted, all quotations from the Bible in this book are drawn from the King

James Version. However, the principles of Analytical Reading apply equally to more modern translations as well as to other types of literature.

A word about interpretation

The moment you have emphasized or subdued, paused or connected, or changed your inflection, you have interpreted. You can't avoid it unless you read in a dreadful monotone. Knowing **where** and **how** to emphasize or pause is what Analytical Reading reveals in this book.

Can you do this?

Sometimes a student may feel a lack of sufficient education to become a good oral reader. Don't let this thought discourage you. A person without much experience can become a more pleasing reader than someone who has had much training in oral reading but has not learned to apply the principles in this book.

The material in this book has been tested over many years. Thousands of students and readers have found it satisfyingly practical.

Yes, you can do this. So let's get started.

PART TWO

Basic Principles of Emphasis

4

Emphasizing New Ideas

My rule for knowing which word to lean on is the word that tells you something new, something that is different from what you expected.

Lewis Carroll, quoted in *Victoria Through the Looking Glass*, Simon and Schuster, Inc., New York

The whole secret of meaningful, and therefore natural, emphasis lies in stressing the word that carries the thought, the "meaning-word" that gives the sense.

When we speak, we naturally emphasize each new idea, and subdue the old. It's automatic. We understand the ideas and don't need to stop and think what words to emphasize or subdue. When you apply this principle of emphasizing new ideas and subduing old ideas to the material you are reading you will sound natural and conversational, and the meaning will be clear. And isn't giving out a clear meaning—giving the sense—most desirable?

Suppose you said to a newly-arrived visitor:

Here is a very comfortable chair. Please, sit in this chair.

Probably you would slightly stress *comfortable* and *chair* in the first sentence. Would you stress *chair* in the second sentence? Certainly not. Try it that way and see how absurd it sounds. [Go ahead. We'll wait.]

You have already introduced the subject of the chair and stressed it. It was the new idea, the "meaning-word," in the first sentence. In the second sentence *chair* is an old idea, something now taken for granted and not worth stressing. But the thing you're now interested in is not the chair but the sitting in it. *Sit* is the new idea and so you emphasize it. We do this by raising the pitch on the accented syllable of the word to be emphasized.

Here is a very **comfortable chair**. Please, **sit** in this chair.

Be sure to go up high enough on the word you decide to stress so you have room to come down. We all have several pitches or tones in our natural speaking voice, so when you stress, go up a couple of tones to prepare for subduing the next word or phrase.

Read these sentences aloud:

Florence is my sister. I love Florence.

Probably you stressed the first *Florence* and *sister*. But surely you didn't stress the second *Florence*, because it is now an old idea. Instead, if you read it naturally, you subdued the second *Florence* and stressed *love*, which is the new idea.

The second *Florence* is an old, taken-for-granted idea. In fact, you would be even more likely to leave it out altogether and substitute the little pronoun *her*.

Florence is my **sister**. I **love** her.

A pronoun is a word with no meaning of its own, independent of the noun it refers to. By derivation and by definition it is merely a word used for a noun. When the meaning of the noun is so obvious that you don't even bother to express it but use instead a mere substitute word, you hardly need to stress the substitute. We don't mean that pronouns are never to be stressed, however. We cover pronouns later in chapter 20.

PRACTICE EXAMPLES

At the end of a chapter you may find examples to practice what has been discussed, followed by suggestions which you may accept or reject as your reason dictates. If this is your personal copy of *Giving the Sense* why not take a pencil and work along with us. Draw a line under the new ideas you would emphasize in the following examples:

1. Then enquired he of them the hour when he began to amend. And they said unto him, Yesterday at the seventh hour the fever left him. (John 4:52)

2. No lion shall be there nor any ravenous beast shall go up thereon, it shall not be found there; (Isaiah 35:9)

3. Dorothy nodded gravely and the Queen made a curtsy, after which she became quite friendly with the little girl. (*The Wizard of Oz*, L. Frank Baum)

4. [5] And the angel answered and said unto the women, Fear not ye: for I know that ye seek Jesus, which was crucified. [6] He is not here: for he is risen, as he said. Come, see the place where the Lord lay. [7] And go quickly, and tell his disciples that he is risen from the dead; (Matthew 28)

5. [23] They that go down to the sea in ships, that do business in great waters; [24] These see the works of the Lord, and his wonders in the deep.
   [29] He maketh the storm a calm, so that the waves thereof are still. [30] Then are they glad because they be quiet: (Psalm 107)

DISCUSSION

1. Since the question contained the word *hour,* the servant, in answering, would subdue *hour* and emphasize *seventh,* the new idea, telling **which** hour. If someone asked you, "At what time of day did it happen?" you would reply, "At **noon**-time", *noon* being the new idea.

2. *Lion* is a new idea, and would be emphasized, but is *ravenous beast* a new idea? Isn't a lion a ravenous beast? If you emphasize *ravenous beast* it sounds as if it is different from *lion,* thus you would not be giving out a true meaning. Isn't the new idea *any,* as opposed to just the one type, a lion. The word *thereon* and the word *there* at the end of the verse, are old ideas, from the word *there* at the beginning of the verse, and don't need emphasis. Isn't *found* the new idea at the end of the verse?

3. Is *the little girl* a new idea? Isn't that Dorothy? So wouldn't the stress go on *friendly?*

4. In the last verse, is *that he is risen from the dead* new? Isn't it all old from verse 6? Isn't the last new idea *disciples*? So wouldn't you need a good stress on *disciples,* going up high enough in pitch so that you could then drop your pitch and subdue the entire phrase *that he is risen from the dead*?

5. In verse 30 would you emphasize *quiet* or *glad?* Isn't *quiet* an old idea after *calm* and *still? Glad* is the new idea. This is also an example of subduing pronouns as each *they* in verse 30 stands for something or someone already mentioned in the verses above. The first *they* is the people that *go down in sea in ships.* The second *they* is *the waves.*

5

Subduing Old Ideas

When Edmond Hillary made the first ascent to the top of Mount Everest, he was only halfway through his journey. He still had to make the arduous descent. When you have emphasized the new idea, you also are only halfway there. There are old ideas that need to be subdued. Just as you raise your pitch on the word or words you decide to emphasize, you must keep your pitch low on the words you decide to subdue. This principle of emphasizing the new idea and subduing the old idea is the basis of meaningful, conversational emphasis.

A director of plays once said to me, "Oh, if I could only get these people to stop reading lines this way: 'I need something from the **library**. Let's go to the **library**.'" Once you've mentioned the library, the word *library* becomes an old idea and you naturally subdue it. In fact, you could just say, "Let's **go** there." If you can actually omit a word, or substitute a more general word without affecting the meaning, why should you emphasize it? Here, wouldn't you stress *go* instead? Isn't *go* the new idea? *Library* is so clearly understood that you might not even need *there* as a substitute word. Couldn't you simply say, "Let's **go**"?

A radio or television announcer aware of this principle would not say, "France and other **European countries**;" "his grandmother and his aunt and many **relatives**;" "apartments, condominiums, and other **domiciles**." A weather newscaster wouldn't tell us about the snow "in New Hampshire and other **New England** areas."

The newscaster would realize that, since France is a European country, *European countries* would be subdued as old; that, since grandmothers and aunts are relatives, *relatives* would be subdued; that, since apartments and condominiums are domiciles, *domiciles* would be subdued. Obviously, the announcer should stress *other* (European countries), *many* (relatives), and *other* (domiciles), respectively, in the three examples. And, of course, the weatherman would emphasize *other*, since New Hampshire is an area of New England, and so *New England areas* is an old idea.

Beware of emphasizing too many words. Some readers think that the more words they emphasize the more meaning they give out and the more convincing it sounds, but emphasizing too many words clutters the meaning of a sentence. Emphasizing too many words is almost as bad as emphasizing the illogical words. If you underscore a few words when writing a letter, you call special attention to those words; but if you underscore all the words you're right back where you started—with no emphasis at all.

This is why you need to devote as much care to subduing as to stressing. Emphasizing too many words steals the thunder from the one word, or the few words, that should be emphasized in order to bring out the writer's point.

Some people can emphasize words easily. Often it is subduing that presents the difficulty. Many will stress a word and then unconsciously go right along and stress the following word, even though it should be subdued. This of course rubs out the emphasis from the preceding word. Again, go up high enough on the word you decide to stress so you have room to come down to prepare for subduing the next word or phrase.

How would you say these sentences?

Do you want fries with that?
There's a drone overhead.
That's a counterfeit bill.

Don't you naturally subdue *with that, overhead, bill*? Those are not the new ideas.

A good test to follow is any word you can leave out without changing the meaning you need not and should not stress:

Do you want fries?
There's a drone.
That's a counterfeit.

PRACTICE EXAMPLES

Okay, take your pencil and draw a line under the new ideas and draw a light squiggly line through the old ideas in the following examples. Then read them out loud according to your markings and see what meaning comes across to the hearer.

1. And it came to pass in those days that [Jesus] went out into a mountain to pray, and continued all night in prayer to God. (Luke 6:12)

2. And he trembling and astonished said, Lord, what wilt thou have me to do? And the Lord said unto him, Arise, and go into the city, and it shall be told thee what thou must do. (Acts 9:6)

3. Almighty God hath created the mind free. All attempts to influence it by temporal punishments or burthens . . . are a departure from the plan of the Holy Author of our religion. (Thomas Jefferson)

4. And the inhabitant shall not say, I am sick: the people that dwell therein shall be forgiven their iniquity. (Isaiah 33:24)

DISCUSSION

1. Is prayer at the end of the verse new? No, so it would be subdued. What about the phrase "to God?" Although those words are not stated elsewhere in the verse, isn't it understood that Jesus would be praying to God? So the emphasis would go on *night,* the last new idea. Couldn't you leave out the last 4 words, and leave the listener with the point—that he prayed all night. Of course, you wouldn't leave anything out of the verse, but by subduing those words, the meaning comes out clearly.

2. Although this is frequently read with some stress on *what thou must do*, doesn't this just clutter the meaning? *What thou must do* is merely a repetition of *what wilt thou have me to do* and, therefore, should not be emphasized. For practice, try reading the verse leaving out the last four words and you will see that the sense does not lose anything really essential.

3. At the end of the quote, is *Holy Author of our religion* a new idea? Isn't it the same thing as *God*? And does the idea that God hath created something imply a *plan*? So wouldn't everything after *departure* be old ideas and therefore subdued?

4. *The people that dwell therein* is surely the same as *the inhabitant* and would be subdued, letting the new ideas, *forgiven* and *iniquity,* stand out clearly.

6

Be Alert to Synonyms

Another thing to watch for is a synonym expressing an old idea. Sometimes an old idea is expressed not by the same word but by a synonym, a word that means almost exactly the same thing.

> On wings of fiction we fly to happier lands; or we lose ourselves just as pleasantly when borne on melody's pinions.

Both *wings* and *fiction* would be emphasized as new ideas, and so would *melody's,* since it is contrasted with *fiction;* but *pinions* certainly should be subdued, since it means the same thing as *wings.* There is no repetition of words here but a repetition of ideas. Try substituting *wings* for *pinions.*

> On wings of fiction we fly to happier lands; or we lose ourselves just as pleasantly when borne on melody's wings.

You naturally subdue the second *wings.* So you should subdue its equivalent, *pinions.*

PRACTICE EXAMPLES

Take out your pencil and see if you can find the synonyms in the following examples:

1. [11] My son, despise not thou the chastening of the Lord;, neither be weary of his correction: [12] For whom the Lord loveth he correcteth; (Proverbs 3)

2. Let that therefore abide in you which ye have heard from the beginning. If that which ye have heard from the beginning shall remain in you, ye also shall continue in the Son, and in the Father. (I John 2:24)

3. A man's name was his personal property. For convenience in calling him up to the bar and in designating him among other blue-shirted bipeds, a temporary appellation, title, or epithet was conferred upon him by the public. (O. Henry, *Christmas by Injunction*)

4. But be not ye called Rabbi: for one is your Master, even Christ; and ye are all brethren. (Matthew 23:8)

5. [1] Blessed are the undefiled in the way, who walk in the law of the Lord. [2] Blessed are they that keep his testimonies, and that seek him with the whole heart.
   [4] Thou hast commanded us to keep thy precepts diligently. (Psalm 119)

DISCUSSION

1. Which is newer in the second phrase, *correction* or *weary*? Isn't *correction* a synonym of *chastening*? So *weary*, the new idea, would be stressed and *correction* subdued. In the final phrase, *loveth* is clearly the new idea and would be stressed; the repeated idea, *correcteth*, would be subdued.

2. In the first sentence, *abide* and *beginning* are new ideas and should be emphasized. In the second sentence "that which ye have heard from the beginning" is clearly a repeat and

can be subdued. What about the word *remain*; is it a new idea or is it the same as *abide*? Isn't the new idea *shall*? In the next phrase, is *continue* a new idea? Or is it a repeat of both *abide* and *remain*? And isn't *shall* also a repeated idea? If you go to the original Greek, you will find that *abide, remain,* and *continue* are all the same word. These synonyms are old ideas and shouldn't be emphasized. If it is difficult to subdue *remain* and *continue* when you are reading, practice the verse using *abide* in each phrase, and your ear will tell you that these are old ideas. *Son* and *Father* at the end of the verse are new ideas, and would be emphasized.

3. Aren't *appellation, title* and *ephithet* all synonyms for *name* here? So they would be subdued, and the new idea, *temporary* would be emphasized.

4. If you look up the word *Rabbi* you will find that it means Master. Therefore, isn't *Master* an old idea, to be subdued, and *one* the new idea, to be emphasized? By subduing the word *Master*, you bring out the otherwise hidden meaning.

5. In verse 2 is *his testimonies* a new idea? Is it a synonym for *the law of the Lord*? In Psalm 119 there are many terms that stand for the word of God—Law, testimonies, precepts, statutes, commandments, judgments. (In all 176 verses there are only 2 that don't contain a term for or description of God's word). While these terms present different aspects of God's word, aren't they used as synonyms? So wouldn't you subdue testimonies in verse 2? What about *keep*? Isn't the idea *keep his testimonies* the same as *walk in the law of the Lord*? Aren't the new ideas in verse 2 *seek* and *whole heart*? Those would be stressed. In verse 4, *thy precepts* is that same idea as *law* and *testimonies*, so would be subdued. Aren't the only new ideas *commanded* and *diligently*?

7

Simple Contrasts

Frequently the "new idea" is more than just a new idea: it is a definite contrast.

> I voted for Elaine, but Philip was the winner.

Elaine and *Philip* are not only both new ideas, aren't they in contrast with each other? Wouldn't you naturally emphasize *Elaine* and *Philip*?

> I think green paint would be better than blue.

Here we are comparing two paints. Wouldn't you emphasize *green* and *blue* as contrasting words?

Degrees of Emphasis

When we indicate that a word would get "more" emphasis or a "heavier" emphasis, that does not mean an increase in volume. It means using a higher pitch on the accented syllable of the stressed word. We all have several tones in our natural speaking voice, and there is more than one level to use for emphasis. There are degrees of stress: We give slight rise in pitch on merely new ideas, more on a contrast.

You don't want to stress the first of a pair of contrasted words as heavily as the second or you will produce the effect of hitting words or plugging, which can become a mannerism annoying to your hearers. You don't have to knock your listeners down to show them you know where the emphasis belongs, and you must give them credit for being able to catch the meaning without having everything heavily underscored for them.

Though both contrasting words are stressed, we give still more stress to the second. In the preceding examples *Philip* receives more stress (higher pitch) than *Elaine*. *Blue* is slightly heavier than *green*. Note how this principle applies to the next example.

> Honesty is the best policy: dishonesty, therefore, should be avoided.

Here *dishonesty* would naturally receive the greatest stress of any word in the sentence, because it is not only a new idea but a pointed contrast to *honesty*.

This emphasizing of the contrast is so natural and automatic in normal conversation that the accent shifts to the particular syllable that brings out the contrast, and we raise the pitch on that syllable. The dictionary pronunciation of *dis**hon**esty* accents the second syllable, as we all do normally. But to accent it that way in this example would be to rob it of sense. Try it aloud that way: **Hon**esty is the best policy: dis**hon**esty, therefore, should be avoided. [We'll wait.] Sounds unnatural, doesn't it?

The syllable *dis-* is the thing that brings out the contrast between *honesty* and ***dis**honesty*. So, in ordinary speech we accent the first syllable of *dishonesty*, since in conversation we are not thinking of dictionaries, spellers, and grammars; we are thinking of the sense. This is how we pronounce words in everyday conversation. We stress a contrasting syllable by raising the pitch of our voice even if it isn't the syllable accented in the dictionary.

Honesty is the best policy: ***dis****honesty, therefore should be avoided.*

Is there more than one contrast pair?

Be alert for contrasts that may not be obvious at first. Sometimes there is more than one pair of contrasts. Consider Matthew 7:3:

> And why beholdest thou the mote that is in thy brother's eye;
> but considerest not the beam that is in thine own eye?

Everyone will see the contrast between *thy* ***brother's*** *eye* and *thine* ***own*** *eye*. Not everyone notices the contrast between ***mote*** (a small particle) and ***beam***.

Similarly in Daniel 3:24-25:

> Did we not cast three men bound into the midst of the fire?
> Behold I see four men loose, walking in the midst of the fire.

Everyone will see the contrast between ***three*** *men* and ***four*** *men*. Not everyone will notice the contrast between ***bound*** and ***loose***.

New and newer ideas: distinctions

We give light stress to merely new ideas, more to distinction that is not quite a contrast. "He has truthfulness and integrity." You give light stress to *truthfulness,* a new idea, heavier to *integrity. Integrity* is not a contrast to *truthfulness,* but is slightly different. You would raise your pitch very slightly on *truth-*(in *truthfulness*), and a bit higher on *–teg-* (in *integrity*).

Different parts of speech contrasted.

Be aware that two contrasting words do not have to be the same part of speech. Don't expect that a noun must be contrasted with a noun, a verb with a verb, etc. It cannot be repeated too often that you are reading ideas, thoughts, meanings, not just words or parts of speech. Read this sentence aloud:

> Among birds the male parent is more likely to accept responsibility than among the four-footed creatures.

Which words did you heavily emphasize? *Parent? Footed?* Or, still worse, *creatures?* That's the way constructions of this type often are stressed, and this reading misses the point almost completely. Try recasting the sentence:

> The male parent among birds is more likely to accept responsibility than among the four-footed creatures.

You see that *birds* (a noun) and *four* (an adjective) are the only words that receive heavy emphasis, since the whole point of the sentence is to contrast the habits of the male parent among **birds** (having two feet) with the male parent among creatures having **four** feet. Stressing *creatures* is pointless, because both kinds of animal are creatures. *Four-footed,* not *creatures,* is the meaning-word, as it is contrasted with *birds* (the two-footed). Since both of these creature types have feet, the part of the *four-footed creatures* that carries the meaning and would be stressed, is *four.*

Implied New or Old Idea; Implied Contrasts.

Just for fun, try reading each of the following examples several times, emphasizing only one noun, one pronoun, or one verb, and a different one each time, and then ask yourself what you are implying in each case.

> I am going to Boston to buy some beans.
> I never said that you stole the money.

How would you read this?

> Some trappers and fishermen were alarmed by the meteor but most citizens didn't even know that it had fallen.

This sentence was read by a news broadcaster with the stress on *citizens*, suggesting that, since *citizens* is stressed, it must be a new idea and that trappers and fishermen therefore, are not citizens. That doesn't make sense. Since it is safe to suppose that trappers and fishermen are citizens, then, by implication, the word *citizens* is an old idea, left over from *trappers* and *fishermen*. Then *most* is a new idea, almost a contrast, by implication, and should be stressed, and *citizens* is implied to be an old idea and should be thrown away (subdued). Try reading the sentence in an expanded form and see whether you don't automatically subdue *citizens* and stress *most* and *know* with a slightly higher stress on *know*.

> Some citizens who were trappers and some citizens who were fishermen were alarmed by the meteor but most citizens didn't even know that it had fallen.

With a little observation and practice you will be surprised to see that you can detect these implied new or old ideas as easily as the clearly expressed ones. You will become so conscious of them that they will almost pop out at you from the printed page and your reading will gain greatly in meaning, even your sight reading. Your listeners will notice something different but most of them won't realize what it was you did (or even did anything) to make your reading natural and understandable. As you apply the principles of Analytical Reading you will see the meaning, and as you understand the meaning and bring it out when you read aloud, your listeners will see the meaning.

It is not going too far to say that the principles of new-and-old ideas and contrasts are the most important things for a reader of the written word to know. Readers who have grasped these, either by being taught them or by discovering them for themselves, say that this has done more than any other one thing to make their reading simpler and more meaningful, more natural. Why? Because they are the deliberate reproduction of the way people talk in everyday conversation. Once you see these principles, they are so obvious that you wonder why you haven't realized them before.

PRACTICE EXAMPLES

Take out your pencil and mark the contrast pairs in the following examples. Remember to be alert to synonyms in the contrasts, comparisons or distinctions.

1. Abhor that which is evil, cleave to that which is good (Romans 12:9)
2. Glory is acquired by virtue but preserved by letters. (Petrarch)
3. It is easier to build strong children than to repair broken men. (Frederick Douglass)
4. I like animals more than most people.

DISCUSSION

1. Do you see a double contrast? Isn't *abhor* contrasted with *cleave*, and *evil* contrasted with *good*? Each pair of contrasts needs to be stressed.
2. Again, a double contrast, so each pair of contrasts: *acquired* and *preserved,* and *virtue* and *letters,* needs to be brought out.

3. Do you see the triple contrast here? *Build/repair, strong/broken,* and *children/men.* To emphasize that many words in this short sentence, you would have to read more slowly. The contrast words in the second half would get heavier stress (higher pitch) than the contrast words in the first half.

4. How would you bring out a contrast here? By stressing *I* and *most?* That would mean that all people like animals, but I like them more than most people do. What if you stressed *animals* and *people*? That would mean that I like animals more than I like most people. Watch what you are implying with your emphasis!!

8

Carry-over

You now know that we emphasize new ideas and subdue old ideas when found together in one or more sentences. But new and old ideas can carry across sentences or passages when reading a compilation of passages, lines of a play or Bible verses. You don't want to read the ideas of one verse and then start the next verse ignoring what came before. The writer or the compiler put these verses or passages together to bring out a larger thought, and you need to read them together as one. We call this principle "Carry-over."

Carry-over is so important that failure to notice and bring it out can wipe out the vital connection. You may possibly bring out a valid meaning in each part but, if you ignore the carry-over, you have missed the point!

Suppose you are reading aloud this citation from Psalm 119:18.

> Open thou mine eyes, that I may behold wondrous things out of thy law.

A logical reading of this verse would be to emphasize *Open, eyes, wondrous* and *law.*

> **Open** thou mine **eyes**, that I may behold **wondrous** things out of thy **law**.

But if you began first by reading the story in II Kings 6 of Elisha surrounded by the army of the King of Syria—where Elisha prays for his fearful servant, "Lord, I pray thee, **open** his **eyes**, that he may **see**," you will see that there is a carry-over in Psalm 119. *Opening eyes* is now old from Elisha's prayer. *Wondrous things* are old from what the young man saw. The carry-over is the contrast between the young man and the petitioner in Psalms. The logical words to emphasize now are *mine* and *I*.

> Lord, I pray thee, **open** his **eyes**, that he may **see.**
>
> Open thou **mine** eyes, that **I** may behold wondrous things.

Failure to use this carry-over of ideas from one passage to another or even from one sentence or phrase to another means only one thing: the reader is not thinking. He does not see the connection himself, and certainly he cannot give it to his hearers. This is one of the most frequent failings of Bible readers; they read each verse as if it had no connection with what has gone before. They speak each verse or sentence as it comes along, producing a chopped effect and compelling the listener either to miss the point or to have to dig out the meaning for himself. Failure to recognize a carry-over can also cause the reader to read past the following passage too quickly, leaving his hearers little time for figuring out the connection and the meaning by themselves.

> Jesus saith unto her, I am the resurrection, and the life: he that believeth in me, though he were dead, yet shall he live. (John 11:25)

These beautiful words of John are often read by themselves, away from the preceding and following verses, and the readers usually and logically emphasize *resurrection*, as well as *life*. Because this verse is read so often by itself and with this same emphasis, people generally emphasize it the same way even when they read it immediately after the preceding verse 24.

> Martha saith unto him, I know that he shall rise again in the resurrection at the last day. (John 11:24)

Following verse 24, isn't *resurrection* now an old idea in verse 25? In this context, isn't *I* the new idea and the word to be emphasized? Try reading it this way, stressing *I* and subduing *resurrection*, and see how it carries over the thought from the preceding verse. You may like it even better to pause after *resurrection*, letting your voice fall, and then start afresh on a new thought, emphasizing *life*.

> [24] Martha saith unto him, I know that he shall rise again in the **resurrection** at the last day. [25] Jesus said unto her, **I** am the resurrection, | and the **life**:

In II Chronicles 16:12, most readers logically stress *not, Lord*, and *physicians*.

> And Asa in the thirty and ninth year of his reign was diseased in his feet, until his disease was exceeding great: yet in his disease he sought **not** to the **Lord**, but to the **physicians**.

They naturally subdue the last *disease*, because it is an old idea. But, if you read this twelfth verse immediately after reading the eighth verse of this same chapter, see how the emphasis shifts in verse 12.

> [8] Were not the Ethiopians and the Lubims a huge host, with very many chariots and horsemen? Yet, because thou didst rely on the Lord, he delivered them into thine hands.

[12] And Asa in the thirty and ninth year of his reign was diseased in his feet, until his disease was exceeding great: yet in his disease he sought not to the Lord, but to the physicians

Verse 8 brings out the fact that in battle Asa relied on the Lord. Verse 12 shows that in his disease he did not; he relied on physicians instead. Then shouldn't you emphasize the new thoughts, the last *disease* and *physicians*, and subdue *Lord*, an old idea? Look at the difference:

No carry-over:
yet in his disease he sought **not** to the **Lord**, but to the **physicians**.

As carry-over:
yet in his **disease** he sought **not** to the Lord, but to the **physicians**.

In these practice examples, you can see there are varied ways to bring out logical meanings in the texts you are reading. The principles of Analytical Reading allow you—encourage you—to look for the writer's meaning **each** time you read. Seeing a carry-over sheds new light on familiar passages. It's not only enlightening, it's fun.

PRACTICE EXAMPLES

1a. What are the new ideas in this verse from James 1:5?

If any of you lack wisdom, let him ask of God, that giveth to all men liberally, and upbraideth not; and it shall be given him.

1b. How would you read the same verse after having just read Proverbs 2:6?

[PROVERBS] For the Lord giveth wisdom: out of his mouth cometh knowledge and understanding.

[JAMES] If any of you lack wisdom, let him ask of God, that giveth to all men liberally, and upbraideth not; and it shall be given him.

1c. Or, how would you read James if you had just read the story of Solomon in I Kings 3:12, where Solomon asks God for wisdom, and God replies,

[I KINGS] I have given thee a wise and an understanding heart:

[JAMES] If any of you lack wisdom, let him ask of God, that giveth to all men liberally, and upbraideth not; and it shall be given him.

2a. Consider Psalm 111:1-3 [*New Revised Standard Version*]

[1] Praise the LORD! I will give thanks to the LORD with my whole heart, in the company of the upright, in the congregation. [2] Great are the works of the LORD, studied by all who delight in them. [3] Full of honor and majesty is his work, and his righteousness endures forever.

2b. Consider Psalm 111:2-3 after reading Ecclesiastics 2:4, 11: [*New Revised Standard Version*]

[4] I made me great works; I built houses and planted vineyards for myself.

[11] Then I considered all that my hands had done and the toil I had spent in doing it, and again, all was vanity and a chasing after wind, and there was nothing to be gained under the sun.

[2] Great are the works of the LORD, studied by all who delight in them. [3] Full of honor and majesty is his work, and his righteousness endures forever.

DISCUSSION

1a. Reading James alone, the new ideas are possibly wisdom, ask, God, liberally, upbraideth, given

If any of you lack **wisdom** let him **ask** of **God,** that giveth to all men **liberally** and **upbraideth** not; and it shall be **given** him.

1b. Reading James just after reading Proverbs 2:6, aren't *wisdom, God* and *giveth* in James now old and shouldn't they be subdued? What is now new is *lack* and *shall.*

If any of you **lack** wisdom, let him **ask** of God, that giveth to all men **liberally** and **upbraideth** not; and it **shall** be given him.

1c. Now, after the passage in I Kings, the reading of the verse in James might be like this:

If any of **you** lack wisdom, let **him** ask of God, that giveth to **all** men liberally and **upbraideth** not; and it shall be given **him.**

(Yes, not only to Solomon but to all men.)

2a. In verse 2, wouldn't *works* be a new idea and emphasized, and *Lord* be an old idea, therefore subdued? In verse 3 wouldn't *His work* all be old, therefore subdued?

[1] Praise the LORD! I will give thanks to the LORD with my whole heart, in the company of the upright, in the congregation. [2] Great are the **works** of the LORD, studied by all who delight in them. [3] Full of **honor** and **majesty** is his work, and his righteousness endures forever.

2b. However, after reading Ecclesiastes 2:4 and 11, wouldn't the emphasis in Psalm 111, verses 2 and 3 change because the context has changed? Aren't we now contrasting the works of the Lord with the works of man? Now the reading of the verses 2 and 3 in Psalm 111 might be:

[2] **Great** are the works of the **LORD**, studied by all who delight in them. [3] Full of **honor** and **majesty** is **his** work, and his righteousness endures forever.

9

Relative Emphasis of Nouns and Adjectives

In the previous chapters we learned that in ordinary English conversation, people tend to stress the new idea or the contrast, and to subdue the old idea. We're now going to see how this principle applies to noun/adjective combinations.

You remember from studying grammar that a noun is the name of a person or a thing, as arm, head, woman, story, New York, waiter, Frances, chair. And an adjective is a word that describes something, as true, funny, lovely, heavy. An adjective modifies a noun, a noun equivalent, or a pronoun, as true story, lovely woman, heavy chair. Sometimes a noun is used as an adjective to modify another noun, as boy baby, head waiter.

Nouns at the end of a grouping

There are two things you need to bear in mind with respect to nouns and adjectives. First, whenever you stress one and subdue the other, you are generally implying a contrast or comparison with the stressed idea. You need to ask yourself whether that contrast or comparison is logical.

Second, there is a conversational pattern in English of emphasizing the last word in a phrase, clause, or sentence even if this emphasis is not strictly logical. Thus, you may feel a bit of tension between the strictly logical stress and conversational pattern of emphasizing the last word in the phrase or clause.

For example, take the sentence, "He's a good man." There's no news in the fact that he's a man, is there? But don't you usually hear it spoken with the emphasis on *man*? It's not emphasized because *man* is a noun, because it is logical to do so, nor as being in contrast with anything. It's emphasized because it is the last word in the sentence.

Similarly, "There was a friendly tone in her voice." Probably most people would emphasize *tone* more than *friendly*. But if someone had just asked if her manner appeared hostile, wouldn't it be both logical and natural to emphasize *friendly* and subdue *tone in her voice*?

So what principle can a reader follow with noun/adjective combinations? Here's what you might adopt as a reasonable practice:

1. Check to see if logic suggests you stress a word that is not the last one in the phrase, clause, or sentence.
2. Read the sentence aloud stressing this word instead of the final one.
3. If this reading sounds forced or stilted, consider staying with the conversational reading—stress the final word.

Remember that if emphasizing a new idea or a contrast doesn't sound conversational—you shouldn't feel forced to use strictly logic. If stressing the last word in a grouping sounds natural to you and doesn't distort the logical meaning, then this emphasis is appropriate and will sound natural.

I will praise thee with my whole heart. (Psalm 138:11)

Is there any implied contrast with just part of my heart? Wouldn't it sound forced and unnatural to stress whole? Doesn't your ear tell you that you would conversationally stress heart?

He maketh me to lie down in green pastures. (Psalm 23:2)

You could think of green pastures as contrasted with brown, dried-out barren pastures, but in the absence of an expressed contrast, don't you think that it's much more natural to stress *pastures*?

What's implied with this reading?

She looked at him with her beautiful **blue** eyes.

What would she be looking with, if not her eyes? *Eyes* is not really a new idea here, but if you subdue it, and stress *blue*, it almost sounds as if she had two or more sets of eyes, and this time she was using her **blue** eyes. (Of course this emphasis might be logical if she had blue contact lenses on that day.)

How would you read the following example?

I can't believe you ate that whole pie by yourself!

Logically we would stress *whole* and subdue *pie*—the whole pie as contrasted with just one piece of it. But conversationally we stress the ending noun, *pie*.

Good reading is both a science and an art. It is based on logic and also natural conversational patterns. The point to be made here is that if your emphasis doesn't sound conversational—if for some reason it doesn't hit your ear right, then remember this conversational tendency. If stressing the last word in a grouping sounds natural to you and doesn't logically distort the meaning, then the emphasis will sound natural to your hearers.

Stop and think of the real meaning

Often you hear *seasons* stressed when someone reads Psalm 16:7:

I will bless the Lord, who hath given me counsel:
My reins also instruct me in the night **seasons**.

Whenever we're instructed, it's in some season, isn't it? But here we're reading about a certain special season: **night** seasons, contrasted, perhaps, with **day** seasons. Once you have thought of this, it will make you very uncomfortable to hear it read with the stress on the less meaningful word, *seasons.*

She standeth in the top of high places, by the way in the places of the paths. (Proverbs 8:2)

Which is newer in *high places,* the adjective or the noun? Aren't we always standing in some sort of place, if we're standing at all? The attention here is focused on **high** places, not **low.** You probably would never think of stressing the second *places* because you would stress the word that carries the meaning, *paths.* Just so, it is natural to emphasize the other new word, *high.*

And the ruler of the synagogue answered with indignation, because that Jesus had healed on the sabbath day (Luke 13:14).

One wonders how anybody could read this with the stress on *day.* Yet it is often read that way, as though the ruler of the synagogue were objecting to his healing on the sabbath **day** rather than on the sabbath **night.** Of course, the implied contrast here is not between sabbath **day** and (implied) sabbath **night**, but between **sabbath** day and (implied) **week** day. Isn't saying ***sab**bath day* just as natural and easy as saying ***Sat**urday*? So here is another place where logical thought requires emphasis on the adjective rather than on the noun.

Unintended meanings are often implied unconsciously when the word *man* is illogically stressed. In Psalm 37:23 we read of "the steps of a good man" as being "ordered by the Lord." If you stress *man*, it makes your readers infer that the steps of a good woman or a good child are entirely different. It's not the fact that the individual is a man but the fact that he is good that is the meaning.

This is true in the thirty-seventh verse of this same chapter, where we are told to:

> Mark the perfect man and behold the upright: for the end of that man is peace. (Psalm 37:37)

Doesn't this mean, not the perfect **man** as contrasted with the perfect **woman**, but the **perfect** man as contrasted with the **imperfect** man?

Next, in "behold the upright" the word *man* is implied, but it's clearly such an old idea that the author didn't even state it. The new idea is *upright*. You could almost leave out the word *man* in the first phrase and the meaning would still be clear—"mark the perfect." Of course you would never leave out any words when you are reading, but you certainly wouldn't want to stress any words that could be left out without changing the meaning.

To summarize, when reading nouns with adjectives, be aware that if you emphasize one and subdue the other, you may be implying a comparison or contrast with something else.

Nouns with little meaning

In almost any language *thing* is a word with little meaning in itself, just a stand-in or an understudy for some word with more character. In fact, you can usually leave out *thing* or *things* without changing the meaning, unless it is used in contrast with a person or an idea. Since this is so, is there, generally, any reason for emphasizing such a colorless word? Almost always it is the adjective modifying the word *thing* or *things* that carries the meaning.

Notice the words *anything, something, everything,* and *nothing.* In their ordinary use would you ever think of accenting the *–thing* parts of these words: any**thing**, some**thing**? No, we accent the meaningful parts: *any, some, every,* and *no.*

In the Bible, these words are often separated, given as two words, but the accent remains the same as if they were a single word.

> Lay not thine hand upon the lad, neither do thou **any** thing unto him. (Genesis 22:12)

> And God saw **every** thing that he had made, and behold it was very good. (Genesis 1:31)

> That ye may be perfect and entire wanting **no**thing. (James 1:4)

In Psalm 107:43 *things* is italicized.

> Whoso is wise, and will observe these *things*, even they shall understand the loving kindness of the Lord.

The italics indicate that *things* was supplied by the translator. It could be omitted without changing or weakening the meaning.

Many other nouns, besides *thing* or *things*, frequently have less meaning than the adjective modifying them. Among them are *points, places, times, conditions, phases, men,* etc.

When the noun carries the meaning

It is not always the adjective that is the new or contrasting idea. The unthinking habit of always stressing adjectives and subduing nouns would be not only annoying, but often misses the meaning. Many times the noun and not the adjective is the meaning-word.

Dreading the climax of all human ills,
The inflammation of his weekly bills.

In these lines from Byron, wouldn't you stress the nouns, *ills* and *bills*, more than their adjectives, *human* and *weekly?* Try leaving out the adjectives. It doesn't change the meaning seriously, does it? Again, any word you can leave out without changing the meaning you need not and should not stress.

He found him in a desert land, and in the waste howling wilderness. (Deuteronomy 32:10)

In verse 10, *desert,* the adjective, carries more meaning than *land,* which really isn't necessary to the complete sense; but you certainly don't want to stress *waste* and *howling* more than *wilderness,* because *wilderness* itself has much meaning.

If I say a word could be omitted, naturally I would mean omitted as you are working with the sentence, not when you are reading it to someone. This trial omission of a word tests its dispensability. But, of course, you put the word back in, subduing it, when actually reading the sentence aloud. I don't mean to suggest changing one word of the Bible, or of anything else you were given to read or act.

When no contrast is implied

Occasionally you will find a place where you shouldn't emphasize either one more than the other or you will imply an opposite that does not exist. If, for instance, you are reading something about "dying mortals," don't heavily stress *dying* and soft-pedal *mortals* or you will suggest that you mean to contrast **dying** mortals with **un**dying mortals. Of course, there are no such things as **un**dying mortals, because the word *mortal* actually means subject to death, since it comes from the Latin root word for *death, mort.*

However, while you're taking care not to say "**dying** mortals," be sure that you don't fall into the opposite blunder of saying "dying **mortals**," with no stress at all on *dying* and much on *mortals.* This would imply that there could be dying immortals, which is impossible, because the word *immortal* means not subject to death, as it comes from the same Latin word for *death* but has the Latin prefix, *im-* (or *in-*) which means *not.*

Then how shall you read such a construction? Without any emphasis at all? No; that would be not only difficult but meaningless. The natural and logical way to read such a construction is to stress the adjective and then to stress the noun a little more: **dying** <u>**mortals**</u>.

Verbs and adverbs

The same combination of logic and conversational pattern applies to the reading of verbs and adverbs. Is one or the other a much newer idea? Is there an implied contrast? Or does the conversational pattern of stressing the last word not only sound natural, but still convey the writer's meaning clearly? Consider Psalm 40:11:

> let thy loving kindness and thy truth continually preserve me.

Isn't *preserve* a new idea? And there is no implied contrast to *continually*—perhaps only sporadically preserving me. So wouldn't the stress logically and naturally fall on *preserve*?

But consider Jesus' response to Simon's answer in Luke 7:43:

> Thou hast rightly judged.

In this case isn't Jesus telling Simon—"right!" Judged just means answered, and is not a new idea. The new idea is that Simon got it right, so *rightly* would get the stress.

All work and no play?

Here is a construction to have a little fun with, if you are fond of words. Readers and speakers, except foreigners who are not quite at home in the English language, seldom make this mistake, but it is amusing to play with the following construction.

In speaking of a **miniature** painter, we mean a painter of miniatures; by an **Italian** professor we mean a professor of the Italian language. But if we reverse the emphasis and speak of a miniature **painter** and an Italian **professor**, we mean a very small person who paints and a professor (of any subject) who is a native of Italy.

See what happens when we reverse the usual emphasis in these expressions: living quarters, sick bed, sleeping car, giant killer, brief case, stumbling block, speeding ticket, milking machines, waiting room, parking meter, ground hog. You can go on making your own list.

Who says proper emphasis isn't important?

PRACTICE EXAMPLES

1. Ye pay tithe of mint and anise and cummin, and have omitted the weightier matters of the law. . . . (Matthew 23:23)

2. We hope this program will be enjoyed by lovers of opera and other forms of music.

3. I have esteemed the words of his mouth more than my necessary food. (Job 23:12)

4. Every man according as he purposeth in his heart; so let him give; not grudgingly, or of necessity; for God loveth a cheerful giver. (II Corinthians 9:7)

5. Flee also youthful lusts: but follow righteousness, faith, charity, peace, with them that call on the Lord out of a pure heart. (II Timothy 2:22)

DISCUSSION

1. Which is newer, the adjective *weightier* or the noun phrase *matters of the law*? Isn't *paying tithes of mint . . .* a matter of the law? So wouldn't you subdue *matters of the law* and stress *weightier*?

2. A famous music critic read this recently on the radio with the stress on *music* giving away the fact that he was reading a prepared script—since no one just speaking—that is, **thinking**—this sentence for the first time would emphasize music. Isn't opera music? You wouldn't stress *music*, because it's an old idea. Shall you stress *forms*? No, because opera is a form of music—another old idea. Stressing *other*, brings out the contrast between opera (one form of music) and other forms of music.

3. Is the writer implying a contrast with unnecessary food? Isn't *food* the contrast with *words of his mouth?* So, wouldn't you stress only the noun, *food,* at the end of the verse?

4. Isn't *giver* at the end of the verse clearly an old idea? And isn't *cheerful* a strong contrast with *grudgingly?* Don't you need to stress *cheerful* and subdue *giver?*

5. Watch the implication with this verse! I*s* the writer warning against just *youthful* lusts? As if old lusts were OK? Or is

he warning against youthful *lusts* in contrast with youthful something else? Don't you need to be careful to stress both the adjective and the noun here, ***youthful lusts*** to avoid giving out an illogical meaning?

10

Common Denominator Construction

The principle that I call Common Denominator (or CD) is an extension of the basic principle of emphasis: that in conversation we tend to stress a new idea and subdue an old idea.

The importance of CD can hardly be overestimated. Once I understood this phase of emphasis, complicated sentences which had been hard to understand suddenly became completely clear to me. Involved sentences which had been difficult to teach by questions and answers alone, have raveled out like silk when I have pointed out to the pupil the presence of Common Denominator.

As one pupil said, "CD is like a flash of lightning! It lights up the whole sentence!"

The fundamental principle

When you hear people say: "No news is good news," have you ever heard anyone emphasize anything but *no* and *good*? Probably not. Although this seems quite illogical when you stop to think about it, since the first *news* is unmistakably a new idea. But see how unnatural it sounds to stress the first *news*. Logical, yes, but it strikes the ear as completely unnatural; so we hear people say: **No** news is **good** news. Why is this? Because the idea of *news* is already old in the thought of the speaker. It is "common" to both *No* and *good*. And when he subdues *news* in each instance, it makes that idea old also in the thought of the listener. The new idea is what you are saying about *news: No* and *good*. These are the words you naturally express.

This emphasis pattern is not just a "conversational idiom." It is that, but it is far more than that. It is a combination of conversation and logic which follows a definite and predictable pattern or principle. And it is appears more frequently than one might imagine. Here is another familiar CD: "My Time is Your Time." Did you hear *Time* subdued?

How would you read this verse from St. Paul's letter to the Galatians?

> If we live in the Spirit, let us also walk in the Spirit.
> (Galatians 5:25)

Don't you just naturally subdue everything except *live* and *walk*, even though the first *in the Spirit* is clearly a new idea? In these examples, *news*, *time*, and *Spirit* are what the speakers are thinking about at the outset. They are already old in the minds of the speakers. The message is what the speakers are going to say about these ideas. These new-idea words always present a contrast, or at least a distinction or comparison; the idea that is already on the speaker's mind is generally expressed in either the same words (as in these examples) or in two words very similar in meaning, or synonyms.

The common denominator is the idea that's already on the speaker's mind. It is so taken for granted that it could almost go without saying. The words that express the cd are naturally subdued in conversation, so should also be subdued when reading aloud—while the contrasts are stressed.

CD can simply lay a sentence bare, and the meaning will be startlingly clear. You will often find that you have not gone to the bottom of the meaning until you have seen this is a CD construction—and brought it out.

Elements of a Common Denominator construction

1. A common denominator, which is stated at least twice
2. Two or more contrasts or comparisons about the common denominator

Emphasis in a Common Denominator construction

In conversation, we *subdue* the words that express the common denominator both times and *emphasize* the *contrast* words.

Read this aloud: 2/9 + 3/9 = 5/9

Didn't you subdue *ninths*, the literal (mathematical) denominator of these fractions, each time? Didn't you stress *2, 3* and *5*, the contrasts to which this (mathematical) denominator is common? If the paper had had only "2/9" written on it, you probably would have said "two **ninths**." But in reading 2/9 + 3/9 = 5/9 your eye saw the whole equation at a glance, and you simultaneously saw that you were going to be working with ninths, contrasting two of them with three of them and five of them. So you got the writer's point instantly and you said: "**Two** ninths plus **three** ninths equals **five** ninths." And your hearers got the point with the first emphasis: "**Two** ninths."

As the reader of the written word—the speaker, actor, broadcaster, or cleric—subdues the words expressing the common denominator as taken for granted by him, these words become taken for granted by the hearers, too. Because this is the way they themselves talk, they get the point.

There are a number of interesting properties or characteristics of this construction. For example, you can often substitute a pronoun for the word or words expressing the common denominator, or at least involve a pronoun in a simplified paraphrase of the common denominator

Here is Galatians 5:25 again:

If we live in the Spirit, let us also walk in the Spirit.

If you are thinking at the very outset of *Spirit* you could say: If we **live** in it, let us also **walk** in it, substituting the pronoun *it* for the common denominator *Spirit* each time. As a pronoun is merely an understudy for a noun, you see how very taken-for-granted the cd is, since you can replace it with a mere pronoun. I press this point so as to keep you aware of the fact that we subdue the cd word or words. Sometimes we could actually leave out one of the cd words; thinking of time, we could say "**My** time is **yours.**"

How would you read this from Matthew 10:8?

Freely ye have received, freely give.

Did you stress anything but *received* and *give*? You can't miss this one! *Freely* is the cd, (stated twice) and *received* and *give* are the contrasts. You may wonder why I am discussing examples that are so easy and apparent, really unmistakable. Well, I'm not trying to insult your intelligence. It's just that I want you to start thinking in CD, so you will be able to see it, and use it when you come to sentences that I guarantee will not be so easily transparent, and thus gain great insights into the writer's meaning.

Imagine you had to read this line in a play:

We were all hoping for rain, and the rain finally came.

If you didn't have the second half of the sentence you might stress the first *rain* as the new idea. But rain is already in the mind of the character and it would sound very unnatural if you stressed the first *rain,* the cd there. You're thinking about rain and so *rain* already is old, and you do not stress it. Instead, you stress what you say about rain—that you were **hoping** for it and it finally **came.**

Here is Romans 6:8:

> Now if we be dead with Christ, we believe that we shall also live with him.

This reading swings on just two words, *dead* and *live*. To stress more is to clutter it. The first *we* and the third *we* form a tiny cd, and so do the synonymous phrases *with Christ* and *with him*. These six words are subdued. *Live* contrasts with *dead*, and are the two words to be stressed.

> We (be) **dead** with Christ—we **live** with him.

Let's recapitulate:

1. The common denominator is expressed at least twice.
2. The contrast is expressed at least twice.
3. Both statements of the common denominator are subdued.
4. The contrast words are emphasized.

When my granddaughter was about four years old, she had reached the interrogative stage. This was very hard to live with. One day my daughter said, "Tina, I wish you wouldn't ask so many questions!" With great dignity, Tina drew herself up to her full three-feet-six and said, "I **ask** a lot because I **think** a lot."

Even a four-year-old uses Common Denominator!

PRACTICE EXAMPLES

1. For if that which is done away was glorious, much more that which remaineth is glorious. (II Corinthians 3:11)

2. For God sent the Son into the world, not to condemn the world, but that the world might be saved through him. (John 3:17 *Revised Standard Version*)

3. Uncle Henry and Aunt Em had a big bed in one corner and Dorothy a little bed in another corner. (L. Frank Baum, *The Wizard of Oz*)

4. One man practicing sportsmanship is far better than a hundred teaching it. (Knute Rockne)

5. For not the hearers of the law are just before God, but the doers of the law shall be justified. (Romans 2:13)

6. Be of good cheer, Paul: for as thou hast testified of me in Jerusalem, so must thou bear witness also at Rome. (Acts 23:11)

DISCUSSION

1. *Glorious,* the idea that is stated twice in the same word, is the common denominator in this verse, so these words would be subdued. The clear contrasts are *done away* and *remaineth;* those words would be stressed.

2. *Saved* at the end of the verse is not only a new idea, but clearly In contrast with *condemn.* Is there a common denominator? Isn't it *world?* So wouldn't you be sure to subdue *world* each time? Is *through him* new at the end? Isn't it old after the idea of God sending his Son. Couldn't you leave off the

last two words without losing any of the meaning? So they don't need to be stressed. To bring out the very big contrast in this verse, you would only stress *condemn* and *saved.*

3. The contrasts are so clear here, it would almost always be read stressing *Uncle Henry, Aunt Em, big,* and *one* in contrast with *Dorothy, little,* and *another.* Probably no one would stress *bed* or *corner* even though they look like new ideas in the first half of the sentence. Those are the words that express the two common denominators. The contrasts are so obvious from the outset, that you naturally stress just the words that bring those out, and subdue the words that express the common denominators.

4. At the end of the verse the word *it* stands for *sportsmanship,* so it is clearly an old idea. Is it a common denominator? Yes, there is a contrast between *practicing* and *teaching.* So you would subdue the words that express the common denominator and stress the contrasts. What about *hundred* at the end of the verse? Isn't that another contrast, with *one?* The common denominator there is *man.* It is only expressed once, but isn't it implied after *hundred?* So, you would just bring out the contrasts, stressing *one* and *hundred* and subduing *man,* and stressing *practicing* and *teaching* and subduing *sportsmanship* and *it.*

5. The construction that includes *not... but...* clearly indicates a contrast. In this verse, *hearers* is in contrast with *doers:* not the **hearers** of the law but the **doers** of the law. Isn't *of the law* a common denominator? Isn't the idea *shall be justified* the same as *are just before God?* All those words express another common denominator and should be subdued. The only two words in the whole verse that need emphasis are the two that bring out the contrast, *hearers* and *doers.*

6. The common denominator idea is not always expressed in the same words, but still there is a twiceness in meaning. Is *bear witness* new? Or is it the same as *testified of me*? Isn't that the common denominator? So those words would be subdued. Isn't the contrast between *Rome* and *Jerusalem*? In this verse, the word *also* is part of the contrast, so it could be lightly stressed along with the two contrasts, *Rome* and *Jerusalem.*

PART THREE

Basic Principles of Phrasing

11

Phrasing—Flashes of Silence—Natural Places to Pause

A phrase is a group of related words that conveys a thought. Almost every sentence contains one or more phrases, and after some of these the reader should pause.

It has been said of a certain nineteenth century British politician, "[He] has occasional flashes of silence which make his conversation perfectly delightful."

A pause serves three purposes. First, it gives the reader an opportunity to breathe. In conversation we breathe comfortably and frequently at the natural phrasing places, the ends of ideas. But sometimes an unpracticed reader fails to breathe at the natural or logical place and then has to stop for breath at an inappropriate point, interrupting the flow of ideas to the listener.

Second, the pause gives the reader an opportunity to look ahead to see what he is to read next. During the pause following the first phrase he is quickly scanning the sentence to the end of the next small thought. These first two functions are for the benefit of the reader.

Third, the pause is for the benefit of the audience: to use the power of silence to separate ideas that don't go together. The audience grasps the meaning during the reader's "flashes of silence". The audience must be given these frequent opportunities also to catch up with the reader's meaning and think about it, or they may be left hopelessly behind. If the reader never paused except at the end of each sentence, his audience would still be pondering the first part of the sentence while he was reading the last word of it. As a rule, the more experienced a reader or a speaker is, the more pauses he uses.

For example have you ever had someone ask you a question when you weren't paying attention and then, during a moment of silence when you were about to ask to have the question repeated, you seemed actually to hear an echo of it and been able to answer it? That illustrates to some extent how your audience "hears" you during your pauses.

Not only does the pause help to bring out the meaning; a well-placed pause sometimes heightens the effect of a reading as nothing else could.

It can be one of the most difficult things for an inexperienced reader or actor to do: Just to pause, to be still, to inhale, perhaps; and to look ahead. Sometimes the director of a play who is having difficulty in getting an actor to pause tells him to count to three silently after a certain word and to count to ten after another.

It is just as important to pause between ideas that do not go together as it is to connect ideas that do go together. Judicious phrasing helps to make a good reader. After conscientious practice of the principles of phrasing given in this book, many readers have found that they could now read passages at sight better than they could previously, even after hours of practice.

Webster's New International Dictionary, Second Edition, as published by G&C Merriam Co., defines the verb *to phrase* as "to pronounce in sense groups." There are many types of sense groups, and there can be no cut-and-dried rule about when to pause after such a group, since good oral reading is not merely a science but also an art. Therefore, it is a good idea for the reader to learn all, or most of, the places at which a pause can be made and then decide for himself which possible pauses he wants or needs to use.

Here are some of the places (many of which overlap) where you might logically pause. At first such a manner of phrasing may seem arbitrary or mechanical to you. But remember, you do not have to pause (and should not pause) at each possible pausing place.

After the subject.

The subject of a sentence is significant. You are introducing it to your listeners, and as in introducing people to each other, it is a good idea to pause after the names of the persons you are introducing: Mrs. Lowell—Mrs. Cabot.

You may pause after the noun or pronoun which is the subject itself:

> That lovely, symmetrical pine tree | is only five years old.

Or you may pause after the complete subject (with all its modifiers):

> The lovely, symmetrical pine tree growing in our next-door neighbor's yard | is only five years old.
>
> The book that you want | is out of print.

Sometimes a reader or speaker pauses after the subject even though it consists of only one word. This is done when you wish to focus attention on the subject or make your statement unusually impressive:

> I | am a free American.
>
> This | is the Columbia Broadcasting System.

Before the verb.

Frequently, pausing after the subject means pausing before the verb, as in sentences given above. But this is not always true:

Such a policy always, invariably, and inevitably | ends in ruin.

After the verb.

I really believe | every word he has said.

Please indicate | first, second, and third choices.

Today's newspapers have announced | that tomorrow will be a holiday.

Before the direct object.

This is frequently the same as pausing after the verb, as above. However, there are many times when this is not true:

I really believe literally | every word he has said.

Please indicate clearly | first, second, and third choices.

Would you mind telling me | why you spoke that way?

He has made for himself | a very original and useful career.

Before the predicate noun, predicate adjective, and similar constructions.

Some of the following examples entail pausing immediately after the verb but some do not:

Next month he will become | the President of our country.
She looks every inch | a duchess.

Before or after a prepositional phrase.

In his heart | he knew that it would never come to pass.

He knew | in his heart | that it would never come to pass.

It will never come to pass, and he knows it | in his heart.

There are numerous other constructions before or after which it is logical to pause but the six just discussed are the simplest on which to begin your practice. Of course, you don't want to pause after every sense group. That would make your reading sound choppy. Whether you pause at a particular point will depend largely on the length of that sense group, and the length of the following sense group; first, to enable you to take a breath, and secondly, to give the listeners an opportunity to take in the meaning.

12

The Misconception of Punctuation

Perhaps the strongest and most prevalent misconception about phrasing is that a good reader must pause for every comma. It would be hard to think of anything further from the truth. If you have been taught this misconception it is important to realize **why** this is not a sound practice and could create pauses that give your listeners the opposite sense of the writer's meaning.

In conversation we don't always pause where a grammarian would place the commas. If you will listen carefully to the way people talk, you will realize that this is true.

Some pauses may need to be longer than other pauses, and a comma does not indicate whether the pause should be a long one or a short hesitation.

Sometimes logic will tell us, even when there is a comma, not to pause at all. You don't look to the punctuation for your phrasing; you look to the punctuation for the **meaning;** then you look to the meaning for the phrasing.

For example, if you try to phrase Bible passages according to punctuation, you will find yourself rather perplexed, because different copies or editions of the King James Version itself vary in the punctuation of the same verses. This proves that you can't depend on punctuation for phrasing.

Or you might not have any punctuation at all. Consider this from Joshua 1:2:

Moses my servant is dead.

- If we read this as it is punctuated (i.e. without a pause) the meaning is at best ambiguous.
- If we pause after *Moses* and not after *servant*, we are giving out a totally illogical meaning since it would sound as though we were talking to Moses, and we know from verse 1 that Moses is dead.
- If we pause after both *Moses* and *servant* this comes closer to the meaning.
- But if we pause only after *servant* this makes the meaning unmistakable.

Also a very long sentence may have no internal punctuation. It would be very hard for you to breathe and for the listeners to follow your meaning if you never paused until reaching the period.

Again, go to the punctuation for **meaning**. We phrase because of the meaning, not because of the punctuation, although we may need to look at the punctuation to find out the meaning.

Most readers find it is necessary to mark the places where they are going to pause. The general habit is to indicate a pause by a comma. This is done, of course, because of the general misconception that the proper place to pause is at a comma. If you are one of those that mark pauses with commas, please break the habit now. This is important. It is a very bad idea to associate the thought of a comma with the thought of a pause, because you are then likely to think of the comma as the cause of the pause. Use almost any other marking you like such as the vertical bars suggested in Chapter 3. When you want to indicate that you are not to pause at all -especially where there is a misplaced comma—you can use a connecting slur above or below the words that are to be connected without pause.

Here is a pause needed where there is no comma:

> There were a king with a large jaw | and a queen with a plain face, on the throne of England.
> (Charles Dickens, *A Tale of Two Cities*)

Here is a pause is implied by the first comma between *St. Giles* and *to search*, where there should be no pause:

> [The] musketeers went into St. Giles_to search for contraband goods, and the mob fired on the musketeers, and the musketeers fired on the mob, and nobody thought any of these occurrences much out of the common way.
> (Charles Dickens, *A Tale of Two Cities*)

13

What Does it Modify or Belong With?

You are going to learn that phrasing is fun. Sometimes a particular expression logically belongs with one part of the sentence and not so much with another part. In conversation, we bring out the meaning by:

1. connecting the expression with what it does belong with
2. disconnecting the expression from what it does not belong with

Consider the sentence:

When night had fallen, as they had planned, they went home.

Doesn't the phrase *as they had planned* belong with *they went home*? Certainly they didn't plan for night to fall, as it would anyway without their help. Therefore, in reading this sentence, wouldn't you pause after *fallen* and connect after *planned*?

When night had fallen | as they had planned they went home.

In Shakespeare's Richard III, the Duke of Clarence tells Brakenbury about his horrible dream and how it frightened him. Brakenbury replies:

I promise you, I am afraid to hear you tell it.

I once heard a prominent actor read this line with no pause after *afraid.* The meaning that this reading conveyed was, "I am afraid for you to tell it to me."

Can this be the meaning? No, because Clarence has already told it to him. Doesn't it mean: "Just hearing you tell it is frightening?" Shouldn't Brakenbury have paused after *afraid*? This alone would have suggested his real meaning, but stressing the second *I* and *tell* and subduing *afraid* would make the meaning unmistakable. "No wonder you were afraid. **I** am afraid, just hearing you **tell** it."

> I promise you, **I** am afraid || to hear you **tell** it

Consider this from Matthew 1:18:

> When as his mother Mary was espoused to Joseph, before they came together, she was found with child of the Holy Ghost.

What does the phrase *before they came together* belong with? What precedes it or what follows it? Is it . . . *espoused to Joseph before they came together?* Or is it . . . *before they came together she was found with child. . .* ? Isn't it the latter? So don't you need to pause after *Joseph,* and connect *together* with *she was found with child?*

> When as his mother Mary was espoused to Joseph, | before they came together_she was found with child of the Holy Ghost.

Certain adverbs, especially the small word *not*, go a long way toward spoiling the reading by persons who do not analyze carefully enough to see what the sentences really mean and, almost as important, what they do not mean. Hearing it read in connection with the part of the sentence it does not belong with is very disconcerting to those listeners who can distinguish the logical way from the illogical. You don't want to underestimate the intelligence of your audience. The test is to see whether *not* modifies what precedes it or what follows.

> There is therefore now no condemnation to them which are in Christ Jesus, who walk not after the flesh, but after the Spirit. (Romans 8:1).

There are two logical ways to read the last ten words and one illogical way. Many readers unconsciously give out the illogical reading; they pause slightly after *not* and do not pause after *walk*. This makes *not* modify *walk*. But is that what the verse is saying? Is it saying that they don't walk? Rather, isn't it saying that they don't walk this way (after the flesh), but they walk that way (after the Spirit)? Therefore, to make this point perfectly clear, you should pause slightly before *not* and make no pause at all after *not*.

Now compare that verse in Romans with the following verse from Ephesians 4:17:

> This I say therefore, and testify in the Lord, that ye henceforth walk not as other Gentiles walk, in the vanity of their mind.

Here *not* modifies the *walk* that precedes it; it does not go with *as other Gentiles* walk. In order to go with what follows it, it has to mean "not this but that"—"not so-and-so but such-and-such." Here it would have to be "not as the Gentiles walk but as somebody else walks." But, if you follow this long sentence to its end at the close of verse 19, you will see that the way the Gentiles walk is not contrasted with the way anybody else walks. It says merely not to walk as they walk. Therefore, you should either pause slightly after *not* or else pause neither before nor after *not*.

Be sure you don't pause before *not*, as this would leave your listeners with a question in their minds: Well, not as the Gentiles walk but as who walks?

> "Do you reside in Barchester, Dr. Grantley?" asked the lady with her sweetest smile. (Anthony Trollope, ***Barchester Towers***)

This sentence should have a comma after *lady*, since *with her sweetest smile* modifies not *lady* but *asked*. Without the comma, it appears as if *with her sweetest smile* refers to the lady instead of the verb *asked*. So, if you depend on punctuation for your phrasing, you would not pause after *lady* and you would indicate, not that she asked with her sweetest smile—but that it was the lady with her sweetest smile.

> "Do you reside in Barchester, Dr. Grantley?" asked the lady | with her sweetest smile.

Let's take a break: Here are some actual newspaper headlines. Where would you pause to bring out the meaning the editors intended?

Tuna Biting Off Washington Coast

British Left Waffles on Falkland Islands

Lawyers Give Poor Free Legal Advice

Robbers Get Three Years in Violin Case

Odds Are Slim Kids Will Get an Inheritance

It is bad manners to break your bread and roll in your soup.
(Richard Lederer, *Anguished English*)

Sign in a window:
WANTED: MAN TO WASH DISHES AND TWO WAITRESSES
(English Well Speeched Here)

PRACTICE EXAMPLES

1. Now when Jesus was risen early the first day of the week, he appeared first to Mary Magdalene. . . . (Mark 16:9)

2. And the Lord God said, It is not good that the man should be alone; I will make him an help meet for him. (Genesis 2:18)

3. Be not forgetful to entertain strangers: for thereby some have entertained angels unawares. (Hebrews 13:2)

4. The street is Pyncheon Street; the house is the old Pyncheon House, and an elm tree, of wide circumference, rooted before the door, is familiar to every town-born child by the title of the Pyncheon elm. (Nathanael Hawthorne, *The House of Seven Gables*)

5. Kills fleas and ticks for three months. (Ad for dog collar)

6. If we should deal out justice only in this world, who would escape? No, it is better to be generous for it gains us gratitude. (Mark Twain)

DISCUSSION

1. If *risen* meant "arose from bed" you would pause after *early* and connect after *risen*. But, in this verse it means "rose from the grave" or "resurrected." Therefore you would pause after *risen*—probably a substantial pause—and connect after *early*. The placing of the pause changes the sense entirely.

2. What does *meet* go with? Is it a "help meet" like "helpmate"? Or is it "meet for him" as fit or suitable for him? Some Bible research can help clarify. In the King James version, the word "meet" means fit or suitable. The Revised Standard

Version gives "a helper fit for him" and Dr.Moffatt's translation is "a helper to suit him." Webster's New World dictionary gives "helpmeet" as a corruption or misreading of the word "helpmate." So in accordance with this scholarship, wouldn't you pause after *help* and connect *meet* with *for him?*

3. Does *unawares* modify *angels?* Is it the angels who are unaware of what they are? Or is it we who are entertaining them who are unaware of what they really are? If so, then *unawares* modifies *entertained.* Since you can't connect *unawares* with what it really goes with, you need to at least separate it from what it doesn't go with, by pausing after *angels.*

4. Is it *every child* titled the Pyncheon elm? Or is it *an elm tree* which has that title? Since it is not the child, you need a good pause after *child.*

5. What does *and ticks* go with? *Kills fleas* or *for three months?* Could be either one, but where you pause—after *fleas* or after *ticks*—makes all the difference!

6. What does *only* go with—*justice* or *in this world?* Doesn't the second sentence indicate that there is a contrast between giving justice alone and giving justice with something else? If so, then don't you need a good pause after *only* in the first sentence?

14

Two Things Logically Connected with a Third

Suppose you were handed this menu at a diner:

We serve sausage or bacon with eggs.

What are your choices for breakfast? Bacon and eggs seems a clear choice, but could you have sausage with eggs? Or is sausage served alone? There is no way to be sure, just looking at the menu. However, if a waiter spoke those words, he could indicate, by his phrasing, whether or not you could order sausage with your eggs.

1. If he said, "We serve sausage [PAUSE] or bacon [PAUSE] with eggs"
   You could have sausage with eggs.
2. If he said "We serve sausage or bacon [PAUSE] with eggs"
   You could have sausage with eggs.
3. Or if he said "We serve sausage or bacon with eggs" [NO PAUSES]
   You could have sausage with eggs.
4. But, if he said "We serve sausage [PAUSE] or bacon with eggs"
   The sausage is served only alone!

This is an example of the construction called "Two Things Logically Connected with a Third" (or simply, Two With a Third) and you will come across it frequently. In the sample sentence, the first thing is the word *sausage*; the second thing is the phrase *or bacon*; and the third thing is the phrase *with eggs*. When you are going to read a sentence with this construction, you have to ask, "Does the first thing logically go with the third thing?" In our sample sentence, you would have to determine whether they serve sausage with eggs. If the first thing **does** logically go with the third thing, (let's say they **do** serve sausage with eggs), there are three ways to phrase the sentence, to bring out that meaning:

1. Pause after the first thing and after the second thing
   We serve sausage | or bacon | with eggs
2. Pause only after the second thing:
   We serve sausage or bacon | with eggs
3. Or no pause at all
   We serve sausage or bacon with eggs.

Consider this verse: Ecclesiastes 12:9:

He gave good heed, and sought out, and set in order many proverbs.

The first thing is *sought out*, the second is *and set in order*, the third is *many proverbs*. Let's try the test: does the first thing go with the third thing? Does it make sense to say he sought out many proverbs? Yes, so this **is** two with a third and there are three ways to phrase this verse to make that meaning clear.

1. Pause after the first and second things:
   He . . . sought out | and set in order | many proverbs.

2. Pause only after the second thing:
   He . . . sought out and set in order | many proverbs.
3. No pause at all
   He . . . sought out and set in order many proverbs.

Suppose you read the verse from Ecclesiastes pausing only after the first thing, *sought out*:

He . . . sought out | and set in order many proverbs.

Now the verb *sought out* has no object. Sought out what? Doesn't it have to go with *many proverbs*? To make that clear, you would choose one of the three phrasing options numbered above.

How do you choose which of these phrasing options to use? Sometimes it depends on the length of the sentence or of the three things. In some cases no pauses at all is not as clear as the other choices. There may be a contrast or distinction between the first and second thing, so you might want to pause after each of them to bring that out.

This construction can consist of two verbs with the same object, two nouns with the same prepositional phrase, two adjectives modifying the same noun, or other parts of speech.

Consider this sentence:

She is a very considerate, and, what's more, a very delightful companion for a long trip.

Companion is the third thing. The two things that are connected with it are a *very considerate* (first thing) and *a very delightful* (second thing).

You would not want to say:

She is a very considerate, | and, what's more, a very delightful companion for a long trip.

A very considerate what? Don't leave her hanging there.

No, the three ways to connect these two things with the third are:

1. She is a very considerate, | and, what's more, a very delightful | companion for a long trip.
2. She is a very considerate, and, what's more, a very delightful | companion for a long trip.
3. She is a very considerate, and, what's more, a very delightful companion for a long trip.

But what if the first thing does NOT go with the third thing? Consider this sentence:

He personalized his style with his choice of shoe and hanky in the breast pocket. (From *Rocky Mountain News*)

The three things are *shoe, and hanky, in the breast pocket.* If you phrase using any of these ways:

1. Pausing after the first and second things:
   He personalized his style with his choice of shoe | and hanky | in the breast pocket
2. Pausing only after the second thing:
   He personalized his style with his choice of shoe and hanky | in the breast pocket
3. No pauses:
   He personalized his style with his choice of shoe and hanky in the breast pocket

Aren't you implying that he puts his shoe in his breast pocket?

When the first thing does **not** go with the third thing, there is only one way to phrase the construction to bring out the meaning: Pause after the first thing and NOT after the second thing:

> He personalized his style with his choice of shoe | and hanky in the breast pocket.

Visualize this setting as described in Luke 2:16:

> And they came with haste, and found Mary, and Joseph, and the babe lying in a manger.

Who was lying in the manger? All three of them, or just the babe? A manger is defined as a box or trough for hay for cattle or horses to eat. Probably not large enough for all three people. If you consider *Mary and Joseph* together as the first thing, does it make sense to put the first thing with the third thing, *lying in a manger*? No, so this is a NOT two with a third construction. Therefore, there is only one way to phrase this to make the meaning clear: pause after *Joseph* and connect after *babe.*

You still start your analysis of the sentence by recognizing the three things that might go together, but if the first does not go with the third, this is a NOT two with a third.

The salient points of this principle

1. When the construction is two with a third, there are three logical ways to read it:
   - Pause after the first and the second thing
   - Pause after the second thing only
   - No pauses

2. When the construction is a ***not*** two with a third, there is only one logical way to read it:
   Pause after the first thing and not after the second thing.

3. The test to determine whether the construction is two with a third is:
   Does the first thing go with the third (or last) thing?

4. When the construction is two with a third, which of the three logical ways you choose to read it will depend largely on the length of each of the three terms. Also, where the first two terms are in contrast with each other, you may want to highlight the contrast by pausing after both things.

5. Since there are two phrasing principles dealing with association (this principle we call Two With a Third and the principle discussed in chapter 13, What does it Modify or Belong With), you need to be clear on when you can apply the logic of the two with a third principle, and when you should instead apply the logic of the more general principle: What Does it Modify or Belong With.

6. You apply the logic and tests of the Two With a Third principle when:

   - The second thing clearly goes with the third but the first thing may or may not go with the third

   - The first two things are the same part of speech (or combinations thereof)—such as two nouns, two verbs, two adjectives, two noun-verb combinations, etc.

   - There is a conjunction between the first two things (there are rare exceptions to this third point).

When you are reading aloud a long sentence with this construction you have to trust to logical thinking and analysis rather than to your ear. You may be surprised at how quickly you can train yourself to look ahead and see this construction. Once you have trained yourself to recognize it and read it the reasonable way, it will sound very unpleasant to you when you hear someone read it the illogical way.

Eventually you will find a more complicated construction, such as:

The bather surveyed and then dived into the water.

Here *the water* is the third thing, connected with the verb *surveyed* (first thing) and with the phrase, *and then dived into,* (second thing). Did you think it was *dived*? Many readers would, and just stop after the two verbs *surveyed* and *dived.*

The bather surveyed | and then dived | into the water.

But this would make it sound as if *into the water* were connected with both *surveyed* and *dived.* It would mean:

The bather surveyed into the water and dived into the water.

The second "thing" is the entire phrase *and dived into.* It is important to determine exactly which words make up each of the three "things." In this sentence, which is a two with a third construction, you might choose to pause slightly only after the second *thing.*

The bather surveyed and then dived into | the water.

There are certain sentences containing this construction which are too ambiguous for the reader to figure out at first sight.

Five hundred of the enemy soldiers were killed or ordered to commit suicide by their officers.

If you phrase a sentence like this one way it means one thing; if another, it means something entirely different. If you make a long pause after *killed* and none at all after *suicide,* you clearly imply that *ordered to commit suicide* goes with *by their officers* but that *were killed* does not; that is, they were either killed in battle, or their officers ordered them to commit suicide. This then is a NOT two with a third construction. The first thing, *killed* does not go with the third thing, *by their officers.* There is only one way to phrase the sentence if it is a *not* two with a third construction: pause after the first thing and not after the second thing.

Five hundred of the enemy soldiers were killed | or ordered to commit suicide by their officers.

On the other hand, if you think this sentence means that their officers either killed them or ordered them to commit suicide, it is a two with a third and you have your choice of two ways to phrase it: You may pause after both *killed* and *suicide,* or you may pause after *suicide* only. You would not choose the third option of no pauses at all when the wording is this ambiguous.

Five hundred of the enemy soldiers were killed | or ordered to commit suicide | by their officers.

Five hundred of the enemy soldiers were killed or ordered to commit suicide | by their officers.

When you run across a sentence with such an easily misunderstood meaning, you must slightly exaggerate your phrasing. When you pause, pause a long time and unmistakably.

When you conclude that there should be no pause, rush along and make sure that your hearers know that you are not pausing.

Sometimes a sentence is so ambiguous that you can't read it intelligently until you have done some research on it.

> And the fourth kingdom shall be as strong as iron: forasmuch as iron breaketh in pieces_and subdueth all things. (Daniel 2:40)

Without either consulting some other Bible translations or going back to the original language, it is almost impossible to discover the meaning here. Obviously it means that iron subdues all things; but does it mean that iron breaks all things in pieces or that iron merely breaks in pieces itself? Dr. Moffatt's translation gives this as: "for, as iron breaks everything to bits and beats it down." Therefore, according to Moffatt, *all things* is the object of *breaketh in pieces* as well as the object of *subdueth.* In order to show this, you should make a long and unmistakable pause after *subdueth* and not pause at all after *breaketh in pieces.*

> And the fourth kingdom shall be as strong as iron: forasmuch as iron breaketh in pieces and subdueth || all things.

Though you have three choices to phrase a construction that is two things with a third, one may ultimately sound better than the other two. For instance in the sentence, "We often correspond with and see them," the meaning is quite clear: We correspond with them and see them. *Them* is the third thing, the object of the first two things, *correspond with* and *see.* But, since the third thing is only a very small pronoun, it would sound peculiar and stilted to pause before *them;* so make no pause at all after either *with* or *see.* Be especially careful that you do not put a pause after *with* and no pause after *see.*

We correspond with_and see_them.

Although such constructions can be very puzzling, logical reasoning usually uncovers the meaning. Even after the meaning is clear to the reader, he still cannot give it to his hearers unless he knows and applies the phrasing principle of Two With a Third.

PRACTICE EXAMPLES

1. And it came to pass, when Jesus had made an end of commanding his twelve disciples, he departed thence to teach and to preach in their cities. (Matthew 11:1)
2. It is good that a man should both hope and quietly wait for the salvation of the Lord. (Lamentations 3:26)
3. Equal laws protecting equal rights are the best guarantee of loyalty and love of country. (James Madison)
4. And be not conformed to this world; but be ye transformed by the renewing of your mind, that ye may prove what is that good, and acceptable, and perfect, will of God. (Romans 12:2)
5. [1] And after six days Jesus taketh Peter, James, and John his brother, and bringeth them up into an high mountain apart, [2] And was transfigured before them: and his face did shine as the sun, and his raiment was white as the light. [3] And, behold, there appeared unto them Moses and Elias talking with him. (Matthew 17:1-3)

DISCUSSION

1. The three things are *to teach, and to preach, in their cities.* Does the first go with the third? If so, then the three phrasing choices for the end of the verse are no pauses, pausing only after *preach* or pausing after *teach* and after *preach.*

2. Does *hope* stand alone here, or does it go with *for the salvation of the Lord?* If you think it goes with *for the salvation of the Lord,* it is a two with a third construction. It might be best then to choose the option of pausing after the first thing , *hope,* and after the second thing, *and quietly wait,* to be sure that the word *for* is connected to *the salvation of the Lord.*

3. The three things here are *loyalty, and love, of country.* Does the first thing go with the third, *loyalty of country?* No, so this is a *not* two with a third and there is only one logical way to phrase the end of the sentence—pause after *loyalty* but not after *love.*

4. Here there are three things—*good, acceptable, and perfect*—connected with a fourth—*will of God.* You might want a good pause after *perfect.*

5. Let's look at verse 3. If you pause after Moses and connect after Elias, who does *him* refer to? Wouldn't it be Moses? Moses, and Elias talking with Moses. But who does the pronoun really refer to? In Mark 9:4 this event is described, and it states clearly "they were talking with **Jesus**." So, going back to Matthew how do you make this clear? Isn't this two with a third? *Moses* is the first thing, *and Elias* is the second thing, *talking with him* is the third thing. The first thing does go with the third thing—it makes sense to say "Moses

talking with him (Jesus). To make the meaning really clear, and to correctly identify the pronoun *him*, wouldn't the best choice for phrasing be to pause only after the second thing, *and Elias?*

There appeared unto them Moses and Elias | talking with him.

15

Restrictive and Nonrestrictive Modifiers

A modifier is a word that describes, or gives information about, the word (generally a noun) being described. Adjectives are examples of modifiers that, in English, usually precede the word they modify. But in this chapter, we will be discussing expressions that follow the words they modify. The words they modify are called *antecedents*.

Suppose someone said to you:

My mother who lives in Spokane | is coming to visit me.

Doesn't this sound as if this person has more than one mother, and that the one who lives in Spokane is coming for a visit?

Then how about this:

My mother | who lives in Spokane | is coming to visit me.

Now we understand the speaker's one and only mother is coming to visit, and by the way, she is coming in from Spokane.

Who lives in Spokane is a modifier in the sentence above. What we need to ask ourselves: Is this modifier essential to the meaning, or is it just additional information? If *who lives in Spokane* is essential to the meaning it is a ***restrictive*** modifier. If it is only additional information about the antecedent, if it is not necessary to define what person or what object is being discussed, it is a ***nonrestrictive*** modifier. Let's check. Is the essential message clear if we leave the modifier out: "My mother is coming to visit me." Yes, so this is a ***non***restrictive modifier, and we set the modifier apart by pauses as in the second illustration above.

A restrictive modifier is one that restricts, confines, or limits the thing or person to one particular thing, person, action, or class. If a modifier is restrictive, it is necessary to the sense of the sentence, so that it cannot be left out without clouding or ruining the meaning.

A nonrestrictive modifier merely gives some additional information about the person or thing that is being spoken of. It does not point out one particular person or thing and may be left out without clouding or ruining the meaning.

There are two tests to apply to determine whether a modifier is restrictive or not:

1. Does the modifier limit the antecedent down to only one person, thing, group, or class? If yes, then it is a restrictive modifier; if no, then it is nonrestrictive.

2. Would the meaning be clear if you omitted the modifier? If yes, then it is a nonrestrictive modifier; if no, then it is restrictive.

In some passages, the first test works better; in other passages, the second test works better. In the sentence:

> The fraternity brother that we just elected president is my roommate,

That we just elected president is a restrictive modifier of *brother*, singling out from all the other fraternity brothers the one and only fraternity brother that "we just elected president." Since a person normally refers to only one mother, no restrictive modifier is needed in the first example; but one has many fraternity brothers (unless one belongs to a very exclusive fraternity, indeed, with only two members!) and, therefore, a restrictive modifier is needed to point out the very one that "we just elected president." Leaving out this restrictive modifier obscures the meaning of the sentence: "The fraternity brother is my roommate" leaves one wondering "Which fraternity brother?"

It is surprising how much meaning can be brought out by such a simple thing as the logical phrasing of restrictive and nonrestrictive modifiers. Also, it is surprising how many experienced readers fail to read them in a way that brings out the intended meaning. It is true that listeners can often piece out the meaning for themselves but they should not be required to do so. Also, while the hearer is busy puzzling about what has just been read, he fails to hear what follows.

The pause is not the effect of the comma. It is the sense that is the cause of the pause.

In such a sentence as "Every citizen that fails to vote is sadly neglecting his duty," leaving out the restrictive modifier *that fails to vote* not only obscures the meaning but completely changes it, leaving a statement that is absolutely untrue. "Every citizen is sadly neglecting his duty" is obviously false.

In writing, nonrestrictive modifiers should be set off by commas. Restrictive modifiers should not be set off by commas, because they are too closely connected, too vital, to the meaning of the word they modify to be separated from it by even a comma. But since you can't depend on the writer to follow this consistently, it is up to you to insert pauses where they logically belong—and to connect without pause when a comma is placed incorrectly. The comma is not the cause of the pause. The pause is not the effect of the comma. It is the **sense** that is the cause of the pause.

To repeat, in reading a sentence containing a restrictive modifier, almost always connect the modifier with the word it modifies, as they are too closely connected to be separated by even a very slight pause.

In reading a sentence containing a nonrestrictive modifier, almost always pause before the nonrestrictive modifier or you will give the impression that it is a restrictive modifier.

These sentences would probably be phrased as follows:

My mother, | who lives in Spokane, | is coming to visit me.

The fraternity brother that we just elected president | is my room-mate.

Every citizen that fails to vote | is sadly neglecting his duty.

Notice that the modifier may be a clause (a group of related words containing a subject and a predicate), as in the examples already discussed, or it may be just a phrase (a group of related words not containing a subject and a predicate), as in the following sentences:

The man in the moon | came down too soon.

His wife | next to the piano | is a well-known columnist.

In the moon is a restrictive modifier, a phrase describing *man*, distinguishing the man in the moon from terrestrial men. But *next to the piano* is a phrase modifying *wife* nonrestrictively. It is thrown in merely to tell something extra about *His wife*, to locate her in the room but not to single her out from all other wives, since he is assumed to have only one wife.

Modifiers separated from their antecedents

Difficulties sometimes come up when a restrictive modifier does not immediately follow its antecedent. Consider this statement:

The character in the book that I like best is the White Knight.

The modifier is *that I like best.* What does it modify? Is it the *book that I like best*? Or is it *the character that I like best*? Wouldn't it be *the character that I like best*? The principle of What Does it Modify or Belong With would indicate a pause after *book.* If you don't pause after *book,* your listeners could be confused. Therefore:

- put a little emphasis on *character* to indicate it as the antecedent
- give a very short pause after *book*
- keep a level inflection at that point.

You only need to do these things where your listeners could be confused if you don't. For example, in the sentence "The days come no more that brought sorrow and destruction," the modifier, *that brought sorrow and destruction,* could not possibly modify *more.* Your listeners would not be confused if you did not pause after *more.*

Consider this sentence:

There was love between [Silas Marner] and the child that blent them into one, and there was love between the child and the world. . . . (George Eliot, *Silas Marner*)

Here it might be a little clearer if you put a little emphasis on *love,* a very short pause after *child,* and keep a level inflection there.

In the following Bible verse, this is even more critical:

And a certain man lame from his mother's womb was laid daily at the gate of the temple which is called Beautiful, to ask alms of them that entered into the temple. (*Acts 3:2*)

Listeners could easily be confused as to whether it was the temple *which is called Beautiful*, or the gate. Verse 10 makes it clear that it was the gate. To make this clear to the listener, the reader should put a little emphasis on *gate*, make a very short pause after *temple* and keep a level inflection at that point.

Once in a while, you will also come across *redundant* modifiers. These are modifiers that contain absolutely no new information; they could be easily left out without changing the sense one iota. But since they are in the text, you have to read them. The way to deal with these modifiers is to:

- subdue the entire modifier (as an old idea)
- connect the modifier to the antecedent (even though the modifier is nonrestrictive)
- stress the antecedent if it is a new idea

Consider Acts 9:36:

This woman was full of good works and almsdeeds which she did.

Which she did has absolutely no new information in it. It can't possibly be restrictive. But the only logical way to read the verse is to stress *almsdeeds*, connect *almsdeeds* to *which* and subdue *which she did.*

PRACTICE EXAMPLES

1. The man that is sitting in the gold chair is going to make a speech. Our President who is sitting next to him will speak later.

2. I am going to call on my twin brother whom I haven't seen for fifteen years.

3. And behold, men brought in a bed a man which was taken with a palsy. (Luke 5:18)

4. For the grace of God that bringeth salvation hath appeared to all men. (Titus 2:11)

5. But when the Pharisees heard it, they said, This fellow doth not cast out devils, but by Beelzebub, the prince of the devils. (Matthew 12:24)

6. And the man said, The woman whom thou gavest to be with me, she gave me of the tree, and I did eat. (Genesis 3:12)

DISCUSSION

1. In the first sentence *that is sitting in the gold chair* is a restrictive modifier of *man.* It should not be set off by commas, and you should not pause after *man.* In the second sentence *who is sitting next to him* is a nonrestrictive modifier, as the person has already been identified as *our President.* You would naturally pause after *our President* and the modifier should be set off by commas.

2. *Whom I haven't seen for fifteen years* is a nonrestrictive modifier of *brother.* Since you can have only one twin brother, there is no need to restrict *twin brother* to the one you haven't seen for fifteen years. You would pause after *brother.*

3. *Which was taken with a palsy* is a restrictive modifier of man, so there would be no pause after *man.* You might want to pause after *bed,* to make it easier to read to the end of the sentence without any more pauses.

4. Is this one kind of *grace of God* in contrast with some other kind? Isn't *that bringeth salvation* nonrestrictive? So even

though there is no comma, wouldn't you pause after *God*? And probably pause after *salvation* as well.

5. Did the Pharisees say he didn't cast out devils? Could you leave out the words *but by Beelzebub the prince of the devils* and read *This fellow doth not cast out devils.* No, they didn't say he didn't cast them out, they said he cast them out only in this particular way. So *by Beelzebub the prince of the devils* is a restrictive modifier and even though there is a comma after the first *devils*, you would not pause there.

6. Is this a particular woman? Yes, it's Eve, the one woman who gave him the apple. But in this setting, how many women were there? Isn't she the only woman in the garden, in fact the only woman at all? You could leave out the modifier and it would still be clear who Adam is referring to "*The woman gave me of the tree.*" So the modifier *whom thou gavest to be with me* is nonrestrictive, and even though there is no comma after *woman,* wouldn't you need a good pause after *woman,* as well as after *me?*"

PART FOUR

More About Emphasis

16

Negatives

To say "never stress a negative" or "always stress a negative" would be to make an arbitrary rule. Rather, when dealing with negatives, we should follow a logical principle or conversational pattern, just as we do everywhere else. About the only time we can use the word *always* or *never* in discussing reading patterns is to say that "we always avoid the use of *always*" or "we never say *never*."

The negative might be considered not only a naturally emphatic word but the most important word in the sentence, since the whole meaning swings on it. If the negative is omitted the whole meaning is reversed. Consider the following sentences:

Seven is not an even number.
Caesar had never heard of New York.
Charlemagne had no radios.
Icebergs—there are none in the Indian Ocean.

Omit the negatives, and you say that seven is an even number, that Caesar had heard of New York, that Charlemagne had radios and that there are icebergs in the Indian Ocean. Yet, strangely enough, we seldom stress a negative in conversation unless it presents a direct contrast. If you say that "Seven is **not** an even number" you imply that someone has just stated that it is. You would only say "Charlemagne had **no** radios" if someone had said "Charlemagne had radios." This pattern—of not emphasizing the negative word—may seem illogical, but it is our conversational practice, and so should be adhered to in reading, since the patterns by which we give the sense in talking are the ones by which we receive the sense when listening.

Negative contrasts

However, this is not to say that we **never** stress negatives. The negative word *never*, emphasized in the immediately preceding sentence, would be stressed because it is in contrast with *seldom* in the preceding paragraph. This contrast is the only reason for stressing this negative word. We do emphasize a negative that presents a direct contrast or a flat contradiction. If you said, "You shall not eat of it," without anything preceding it, you would probably emphasize *eat* rather than *not*.

But consider these verses from Genesis 2:

> [16] And the Lord God commanded the man, saying, Of every tree of the garden thou mayest freely eat: [17] But of the tree of the knowledge of good and evil, thou shalt not eat of it.

Here, *not* is in strong contrast with the first *eat*. *Eat of it* is so old that these three words could be omitted without changing the sense, and the sentence could end with the stressed *not*.

"Show me thy humble heart, and not thy knee," says York in *Richard II* (II, iv). *Knee* is contrasted with *heart*, and *not* is a contrast:

> Show me thy humble **heart**; do **not** show me thy **knee**.

Negative prefixes

This pattern—of not stressing negatives unless they are pointed contrasts—applies also when the negative is not a whole word but merely a prefix. People say, "Unaccustomed as I am to public speaking. . . ." No one would say ***Un**accustomed* unless someone had just remarked that he was accustomed.

Patricia was fined $50 for non**compliance** with the regulations.

But if you preceded this sentence with: The whole department was complimented for complying with the new regulations. The only exception was Patricia, then you would emphasize *non.*

She was fined $50 for **non**compliance with them.

Consider this about Roger:

Roger was often quite disagreeable.

You would stress *disagreeable* as a new idea, with the accent on *gree.* But if you had this whole sentence, the accent on *disagreeable* would change to the prefix *dis:*

Sally was always friendly, but Roger was often quite **dis**agreeable.

We may conclude, then, that a negative word or prefix is almost never emphasized unless it carries a strong contrast or flat contradiction. ("You are." "I'm **not**." "Yes you are." "I'm **not**.")

Although, as we have just seen, we do not as generally stress the negative word when just talking, we do usually place the accent on the negative parts of *nowhere, no one, nobody,* and *nothing*. In the last two of these, each noun is almost as meaningless as the indefinite pronoun *one* in *no one.*

Negative suffixes

You probably would not say:

> This machine makes too much racket; I want a noise**less** model.

Even if the sentence hit you over the head with an unmistakable contrast you still wouldn't emphasize *less* in *noiseless*. You would scarcely say this:

> This machine is too **nois**y; I want a noise**less** model

In each case you would probably accent the first syllable of *noiseless* even though *noise* is an old idea:

> This machine is too **nois**y; I want a **noise**less model

We can infer then that in spontaneous conversation we usually do not emphasize a negative suffix, even if it is a direct contrast or contradiction. Only in a most unusual and extreme case would we do so.

Another instance of our unconscious resistance to stressing contrasting suffixes, negative or otherwise, even when they present flat contradictions, is this:

> My daddy knows more than your daddy knows.
> He **does**n't.
> He **does**.
> He **does**n't.

In the negative word *doesn't*, it is *does* that would be stressed, rather than the negative part, *n't*. That is, not only wouldn't we stress the negative part, but we wouldn't even say it in its entirety. Instead, we'd be using a contracted form—and it is almost impossible to stress a syllable lacking a vowel sound.

Her soulful interpretation of the sonata was much enjoyed after the soulless rendition by the orchestra.

We'd be more likely to contrast ***soul**ful* with ***soul**less* than *soul**ful*** with *soul**less***. This tendency not to emphasize the negative suffix is purely a conversational idiom, which we follow even when it collides with logic.

Negative following a verb

Besides heavily stressing the negative when it is a strong contrast, there is one other time when we usually stress it. The word *not* receives a light emphasis when it follows the verb which it modifies. This practice is not attributable to common conversational patterns, as we seldom find this word order except in biblical or poetic language or after a form of the verb *to be.*

Tell me not in mournful numbers
Life is but an empty dream.

Even if Longfellow's rhythm did not urge us to emphasize *not*, the sense would. If it read: Do not tell me, it would be natural to subdue *not*, or not to stress it as much as *tell.* It would be even more likely that we would leave it out (by contracting it) and say simply "Don't tell me in mournful numbers." But when we say "tell me not," we emphasize *not* almost as much as *tell.*

Consider Luke 9:

[49] And John answered and said, Master, we saw one casting out devils in thy name; and we forbad him, because he followeth not with us. [50] And Jesus said unto him, Forbid him not: for he that is not against us is for us.

These verses have three negatives, each of which is handled differently. The first could be lightly stressed, the second—as a contradiction—more heavily stressed, and the third completely subdued.

> We forbad him, because he followeth **not** with us.
> And Jesus said unto him, Forbid him **not**:
> for he that is not **against** us is **for** us.

The conversational pattern we call "Sugar"

Suppose that your neighbor suddenly appears at the door and asks if she can borrow a cup of sugar. You go to your kitchen and find that you, too, don't have a grain of sugar left. What would you say to her? "I don't have any sugar." Or possibly, "I have no sugar." Or perhaps "There is no sugar."

How would you emphasize these words? Well, *sugar* is old in all three replies, and *no* (or *not*) is the big contrast, isn't it? *Sugar* is contrasted with *no* sugar. Therefore, it would be logical to stress *don't* or *no*, in each sentence and to subdue *sugar, have* and *is*. Quite logical, yes, but doesn't your ear tell you that you would really stress *have* and *is*, and subdue the *no* in each case? *There is **no** sugar* doesn't sound like speech. *There **is** no sugar* sounds perfectly natural. So does *I **have** no sugar,* or *I don't **have** any sugar.* This emphasis pattern is merely one of the daffy doings of the English language.

When we have an old idea, a negative word, and a verb, we tend to subdue the old idea and the negative and to emphasize the verb.

All this leads me to a diverting theory that I've been playing around with: the possibility that the urge to use the Sugar pattern may account for the large number of contractions of negatives that we find in the English language: *doesn't, haven't, wouldn't, didn't,* etc.

> Then the presidents and princes sought to find occasion against Daniel concerning the kingdom, but they could find none occasion or fault; (Daniel 6:4)

To stress *none* and subdue *occasion* and *fault* would get the idea across but it wouldn't be conversational. *Occasion* or *fault* is the old idea, *none* is the negative and *find* is the verb. Doesn't it sound more like talking if you stress the second *find* and subdue the other two ingredients for Sugar?

> Then the presidents and princes sought to find occasion against Daniel concerning the kingdom, but they could **find** none occasion or fault;

I don't mean to imply that your hearers won't be able to figure out what you mean if you say "There is **no** sugar." Of course, they can, but it won't sound as comfortable to them as it would if you read it the way they would say it. Notice how often this pattern occurs; you may be surprised at the high sugar content of almost everything you read!

PRACTICE EXAMPLES

1. [16] Jesus saith unto her, Go, call thy husband, and come hither. 17] The woman answered and said, I have no husband. (John 4)

2. They have healed the hurt of . . . my people slightly, saying Peace, peace; when there is no peace. (Jeremiah 8:11)

3. They have forsaken me the fountain of living waters and hewed them out cisterns, broken cisterns, that can hold no water. (Jeremiah 2:13)

DISCUSSION

1. At the end of her response, *husband* is an old idea, and the logical new idea might be *no.* But isn't it much more natural to emphasize *have*? Today she might say "I don't **have** a husband."

2. At the end of the verse, *peace* is clearly an old idea and would be subdued; the new idea is *no* but don't you naturally—and conversationally—stress the verb, *is?*

3. At the end of the verse, isn't *water* an old idea, after *living waters* earlier? So it would seem the contrast to a *fountain* of water would be **no** water. Logical, yes, but not conversational. In conversation, the natural stress would be on ***hold.*** Cisterns that can't **hold** water.

17

Potential to Actual

How would you read the following?

> I said "Do it," and he did it.

Didn't you emphasize *do* and *did*? This is a natural contrast from a potential action to an actual action. What if the potential and actual words were the same as in this verse from Exodus 4:3?

> And he said, "Cast it on the ground." And he cast it on the ground.

The second *cast* may look like an old idea, but it is a change of mood (from imperative to indicative) and tense (from present to past) forming a contrast—and therefore would be emphasized as a new idea.

How would you read Revelation 10:10?

> And I took the little book out of the angel's hand, and ate it up; and it was in my mouth sweet as honey: and as soon as I had eaten it, my belly was bitter.

Probably you placed only a small amount of stress on *took* and *ate* and stressed *up* rather heavily; more than likely you emphasized *mouth, sweet, honey, belly,* and *bitter*. This reading is logical. This time read Revelation 10:9 first, and then the tenth verse.

> [9] And I went unto the angel, and said unto him, Give me the little book. And he said unto me, Take it, and eat it up; and it shall make thy belly bitter; but it shall be in thy mouth sweet as honey. [10] And I took the little book out of the angel's hand, and ate it up; and it was in my mouth sweet as honey: and as soon as I had eaten it, my belly was bitter.

If you read it verse 10 with the same emphasis you used before, you are separating it completely from verse 9, merely feeding your listeners a disconnected verse at a time. Now in verse 10 try stressing each *was* and soft-pedaling *mouth, sweet, honey, belly,* and, *bitter*. This gives the idea that it **was** as the angel said it would be. Some readers might like to emphasize *took* and *ate* and subdue *up* in verse 10. This suggests the obvious meaning that I **did** take the book and I **did** eat it up.

18

Appositives

Some readers try to subdue any word which is a synonym of some word just read. They reason that any synonym, being naturally an old idea, should be subdued. There are exceptions.

An appositive is a noun or phrase that renames another noun. It is nearly always placed immediately after the other word. This other word is called its antecedent. These two words are said to be in apposition with each other. Even though this makes the appositive in a sense an old idea, we naturally stress appositives because they identify the antecedent in a new way. This is what we naturally do in conversation, when the antecedent is a new idea.

The Governor, his father, is very popular.

Governor = the antecedent
Father = the appositive (identifying the governor)

If *Governor* is a new idea, it would be stressed, and the appositive, *father* would also be stressed, because it identifies *Governor,* giving a different aspect of the same man. If you stressed *Governor* but subdued *father*, you would imply that he has more than one father (The Governor, his father, in contrast to his other father or fathers.)

If you speak of George Washington, a great general, our country's first president, you will agree that *general* and *president* are synonyms of *George Washington*. So you might argue that, since *general* and *president* mean the same as *George Washington*, they are old ideas and should be subdued; but as appositives they identify different aspects of Washington. Therefore, you would give a light new-idea emphasis to *general* and also to *president*. There is also a slight pause between the antecedent and the appositive.

It's important when reading appositives to use the same inflection on the appositive as on the antecedent; otherwise you will confuse your listeners. This is especially true when there is more than one appositive.

> And Joseph was brought down to Egypt; and Potiphar, an officer of Pharaoh, captain of the guard, an Egyptian, bought him. . . . (Genesis 39:1)

Here the antecedent is Potiphar, with three following appositives. Each appositive tells something new about him, so each is slightly stressed, and each has the same inflection as the inflection at the end of the word *Potiphar*—slightly rising.

PRACTICE EXAMPLES

1. But one of the young men told Abigail, Nabal's wife, saying Behold . . . (I Samuel 25:14)
2. I am the Lord thy God, the Holy One of Israel, thy Saviour: (Isaiah 43:3)

DISCUSSION

1. *Abigail* is a new idea here, and would get a slight stress; the appositive, *Nabal's wife*, would also get a light stress, and there would be a slight pause between them.

2. Here there are two appositives referring to God; each gives a new aspect, and would be stressed with a slight pause before each appositive.

19

Tail of the Kite Constructions

The Tail of the Kite construction refers to a series of two or more new ideas which, taken together, mean only one thing. Conversationally, we emphasize only the **last** new idea.

How would you say this phrase:

Tail of the kite.

Was it **tail** of the kite? or perhaps tail of the **kite**? Or even, **tail** of the **kite**? Probably, most people would say "tail of the **kite.**"

If you are flying a kite, do you work to get the tail up in the air? Don't you rather put your whole effort into getting the kite up? If you do that, the tail automatically goes up. Similarly, the last new idea is like the kite.

Let us go unto the house of the Lord. (Psalm 122:1)

In the absence of some particular carry-over, wouldn't you naturally stress *Lord*? True, both *house* and *Lord* are new, but we don't necessarily stress every new idea in conversation. Isn't the phrase *house of the Lord* just one idea? Let say *Lord* is the kite, and *house* is the tail. Therefore, if you stress *Lord*, doesn't *house* come right along with it, needing no extra attention? If you stress both *house* and *Lord*, that would give a heavy effect.

Here is another example of Tail of the Kite from Exodus 1:1:

> Now these are the names of the children of Israel which came from Egypt

Isn't *children of Israel* all one idea? So you would only need to stress *Israel*.

Most (but not all) Tail of the Kite constructions involve a noun and a prepositional phrase such as *dust of the* ***ground*** from Genesis 2:7.

Biblical examples not involving a prepositional phrase include those with two verbs or two nouns:

> I will come and **heal** him (Matthew 8:7)
> Ye shall go and **pray** unto me (Jeramiah 29:12)
> Flesh and **blood** hath not revealed it (Matthew 16:17)

Idiomatic expressions

Some idiomatic expressions have become so crystallized, in English and in other languages, that the words taken separately do not have any meaning. Expressions like *from day to day* and *from everlasting to everlasting* are in this class. They have become almost one word and it would be foolish to reason that you must stress each *to* as contrasts, and subdue the second *day* and the second *everlasting* as old ideas. The only sensible way to read them is the way they are always read, with each *day* and each *everlasting* emphasized, the second of each with a slightly higher pitch, and with the prepositions subdued. Unless there is some unusual reason for doing otherwise, it is sensible to say simply ***thick****-and-****thin****,* ***ups****-and-****downs***, etc.

20

Different Parts of Speech

The problem pronoun

Some people may feel that Analytical Reading causes one to emphasize too many pronouns, when they hear very familiar readings, such as Shakespeare, the Bible, or the Gettysburg Address. But what the analytical reader is really doing is stressing different pronouns from the ones the listeners are used to hearing stressed. Using the principles of Analytical Reading, will in fact, result in **fewer** words (of whatever part of speech) emphasized. The different emphasis brings out new ideas or contrasts not thought of before.

People who follow the principle of stressing a pronoun that brings out a contrast, and of subduing a pronoun that is an old idea, often hear comments like, "I've never heard that sentence read that way before. Now I understand the **meaning**!"

When you are acting in a familiar play, or reading other familiar material, be very selective about which pronouns you do stress. Before emphasizing or subduing any pronoun (or any other part of speech), just ask yourself: Why? The logic of your emphasis must be so clear, that the hearer will understand the meaning and not be distracted by the mechanics.

As an illustration of why it is unavoidable to stress some pronouns, consider this prayer of Jesus:

> Not my will but thine be done. (Luke 22:42)

Here you have two pronouns, *my* and *thine*. If you don't stress them, what becomes of the rest of the sentence? If you don't say, "Not **my** will but **thine** be done," what's left here? Isn't it inevitable that you have no choice but to stress both pronouns?

It would be equally illogical (and unnatural and unconversational) if someone should say that you should stress every pronoun. For instance try stressing every pronoun in this from Matthew 1:24, 25.

> [24] Then Joseph being raised from sleep did as the angel of the Lord had bidden **him**, and took unto **him his** wife: [25] and knew **her** not till **she** had brought **her** firstborn son: and **he** called **his** name Jesus.

Those hot-tempered verbs

In *Through the Looking-Glass*, Lewis Carroll writes about a talk that Alice had with Humpty Dumpty, in which he discussed how he chose and managed words. This is what Humpty Dumpty said about verbs:

> *They've a temper, some of them—particularly verbs. They're the proudest—adjectives you can do anything with, but not verbs—however,* ***I*** *can manage the whole lot of them!*

Whether or not Humpty Dumpty was just when he accused verbs of having strong tempers, verbs do cause controversy among students and teachers of line-reading and other forms of oral reading. One bit of advice I have heard is, "Stress every verb. Verbs are the action words."

Well, first of all, who says that action is what you are looking for in the passage or play you are reading? That question alone might rule out a need for stressing all the verbs. Perhaps you are reading a page in which someone is trying to soothe a group of frightened people, or maybe trying to put a baby to sleep. Would you need to stress the action words? (**Calm** down. **Go** to sleep?)

Remember the definition that many of us were taught in grade school? "A verb is a word that expresses action, being, or a state of being." *To be* is a verb, but it certainly does not express action. *To sleep* is as much a verb as *to explode. To lie* is as much a verb as *to leap*. So how can a verb always express action? Try to stress every verb in a whole page. Has each verb always brought out a great deal of action? More significantly, have you brought out any meaning?

How can we tell whether a verb should or should not be stressed? Simply apply the basic principles of emphasis: stress the new idea or the contrast; subdue the old idea. Does the verb present a new idea? If not, feel free to subdue it.

Try emphasizing all the verbs in the following from Mark 5:24, 26:

> And a certain woman, which **had** an issue of blood twelve years,
> When she **had heard** of Jesus, **came** in the press behind, and **touched** his garment.

Doesn't it sounds forced? Now try another arrangement of stress in verse 26. Wouldn't the noun *Jesus* get as much or more stress than *had heard*? And doesn't the idea of the *press behind* have more meaning than *came*? Doesn't *garment* have as much meaning as *touched*? You might want just a light stress on *touched*, then more on *garment*.

> When she had heard of **Jesus**, came in the **press behind**, and touched his **garment**.

If you feel satisfied that stressing a certain word brings out a new idea or contrast, then stress it regardless of what part of speech it may be.

Some readers believe stressing of verbs gives strength to their reading. **Meaning** gives strength to a reading. You can't make a mechanical rule about which part of speech to emphasize; all you can do is to listen to people talk. When you do that, you will notice that often it is adjectives and nouns that receive stress rather than verbs. Therefore, avoid making a practice of deliberately hitting all the verbs for no special reason.

21

Naturally Emphatic Words

For some readers, there is an almost irresistible temptation to emphasize words like *all, must, if, should.* These naturally emphatic words do not require extra emphasis unless the meaning specifically calls for it—that is, where there is a contrast, either explicit or implied, or perhaps if there are no new ideas which could take the emphasis. Words like these inherently carry with them enough emphasis, so additional emphasis by the reader is unnecessary. Therefore it is a good idea to look carefully at them and not give them extra emphasis unless they need it.

In this chapter, we'll look at many of these words and see if we can point out the infrequent instances when they might require extra emphasis.

Conjunctions—and, or, but, if

and

Some readers are very much in love with this word and happily stress it almost every time it appears, under the serene impression that they are strengthening the meaning. In reality, such a stress often implies the very opposite of the meaning. Consider Matthew 6:24:

> Ye cannot serve God and mammon.

In this verse some readers like to stress *God and* while subduing *mammon*. But if you do this, aren't you implying that it's just fine to serve mammon, but you must not serve God **and** mammon. Do you think this is a logical interpretation of what Jesus was saying?

On the other hand, if you say that you can't serve God and **mammon**, then aren't you implying that you are to serve God, but not God and something else? In this verse, isn't it critical to stress *mammon*. You may want a lesser emphasis on *and*, but not at the expense of losing the emphasis on *mammon*.

The word *and* may require emphasis if it connects either an old idea and a new idea, or two old ideas, such as in Ruth 1.

> [3] And Elimelech Naomi's husband died; and she was left, and her two sons. . . .
> [5] And Mahlon and Chilion died also both of them; and the woman was left of her two sons **and** her husband.

In this chapter, we have learned that Naomi lost first, her husband, and then, her two sons. So in the last part of verse 5, the word *and* connects two old ideas, which would be subdued; therefore *and* could be emphasized. However, the other six times the word *and* occurs in these verses, there would be no reason to give it any emphasis.

or

The word *or* may connect two very different things, or two very similar things. Where it connects two different things there are instances where a reader might emphasize *or*. For instance, Job 13:22 says:

> Then call thou, and I will answer: or let me speak, and answer thou me.

Think what this verse is saying. Isn't Job saying essentially, "If **you** speak, then **I** will answer **you**; or, you can let **me** speak (first), and **you** can answer **me**." So in this verse, the conjunction *or* is connecting two opposite things, and a reader may want to stress *or* and make a pause after it.

but

This word rarely needs emphasis unless it is introducing a momentous contrast and the reader feels a need to give that contrast an extra wallop. Here is a wallop in II Kings 5:1:

> Now Naaman, captain of the host of the king of Syria, was a great man with his master, and honourable, because by him the Lord had given deliverance unto Syria: he was also a mighty man in valour, but he was a leper.

In this verse, there are several descriptions bringing out Naaman's good points: great, honourable, mighty in valour. But at the end you learn something quite different: he was a leper. Isn't *but* in this case indicating a substantial contrast between his good and bad points? Then you might want to place some emphasis on *but*.

if

Readers often want to punch *if* really hard. This word normally does not require stress. The only times when a reader might emphasize *if* are:

- where the *if* clause follows the main clause and one can logically substitute *provided that* for the word *if*
- where the word *if* is immediately followed by a parenthetical expression
- where everything in the *if* clause is an old idea

John 8 is an example where everything in the *if* clause is an old idea:

> [15] Ye judge after the flesh; I judge no man. [16] And yet if I judge, my judgment is true:

In verse 16, *I judge* is old. Therefore, the reader is almost forced to emphasize *if.*

I Timothy 1:8 is an example where you can logically substitute *provided that:*

> But we know that the law is good, if a man use it lawfully;

In this verse, the *if* clause follows the main clause, and it would make sense to use the words *provided that* for *if.* This would be another of the rare places where a reader might want to emphasize *if.* But the verse could also be logically read without such an emphasis.

Auxiliary Verbs—must, should, may

must

Some readers think they need to stress every *must.* But consider Acts 4:12:

> There is none other name under heaven given among men, whereby we must be saved.

Does this mean whereby we are required to be saved? Or does it mean whereby we may be saved? Isn't this a pretty weak *must,* requiring no stress?

should and ought

These words need no special emphasis, except when there's a contrast between what *is* and what *should be*. In Hebrews 5:12 we read:

> For when for the time ye ought to be teachers, ye have need that one teach you again which be the first principles of the oracles of God;

Since there appears to be here a contrast between what should have been and what actually was, and there is a tone of reproach, a reader might want to emphasize *ought*. You **should** be teachers by now, but instead you still need someone to teach **you**!

On the other hand, when the viper hung on Paul's hand and he shook it off without harm, Acts 28:6 reports:

> Howbeit they looked when he should have swollen, or fallen down dead suddenly: but after they had looked a great while, and saw no harm come to him, they changed their minds, and said that he was a god.

Some readers emphasize the *should* in this verse. It's such a strong emphatic word that they feel they must give it even more force. But does the verse mean that the people felt that he really was obligated to swell up and fall dead? Doesn't it mean merely that the people expected him to do so? There would be no reason here to emphasize *should*.

may

One of the rare times when may could be stressed is when there is a contrast with *may not* or *shall not:*

> The Lamberts **may** come to the meeting tonight, or they may **not**.

Here is such an example from Genesis 3:

> [1] And [the serpent] said unto the woman, Yea, hath God said, Ye shall not eat of every tree of the garden? [2] And the woman said unto the serpent, We **may** eat of the fruit of the trees of the garden:

Here Eve is contradicting the serpent's claim that they were forbidden to eat from any of the trees in the garden. In this case, wouldn't emphasizing *may* be a possibility? And isn't everything after the word *may* old? Here again is an old idea. And what do we do with that? Subdue!

Adjectives—only, any, all, every

only (used as either an adjective or an adverb)

The word *only* rarely requires emphasis, unless it gives the sense of the *one and only*. Sometimes, when *only* follows what it modifies, it may take a light stress, but the reader needs to be careful not to detract from the main contrast or new idea. Consider Matthew 8:8:

> The centurion answered and said, Lord, I am not worthy that thou shouldest come under my roof: but speak the word only, and my servant shall be healed.

Here, *only* follows what it modifies, *speak the word*. It could take a light emphasis but not at the expense of the emphasis on *word*.

any

There is usually not a reason for stressing *any* unless it's a carry-over or contrast as in the following from Isaiah 35:9:

> No lion shall be there, nor **any** ravenous beast shall go up thereon.

all and every

An emphasis on either of these words implies a contrast with *none, some,* or *a part of.* If such a contrast exists, a reader could stress *all* or *every.* In most cases, there is no reason to emphasize these words. In II Corinthians 9:8 we read:

> And God is able to make all grace abound toward you; that ye, always having all sufficiency in all things, may abound to every good work.

This verse abounds with naturally emphatic words: *all* occurring three times; *always, every,* and *may.* In the absence of any special carry-over, wouldn't all these naturally emphatic words be subdued? Instead, wouldn't the new ideas be emphasized: *grace, abound* (first occurrence), *sufficiency,* and *good work?*

Adverbs—also, again, always, ever, never

also

In modern English, the word *also* is generally meaningful, but in the King James Version of the Bible, the word often could be left out without losing the meaning. Consider II Corinthians 6: 1:

> We then, as workers together with him, beseech you also that ye receive not the grace of God in vain.

Since Paul has not pleaded with anyone else not to receive the grace of God in vain, isn't this *also* meaningless? Therefore, it should be subdued.

But Colossians 3:4:

> When Christ, who is our life, shall appear, then shall ye also appear with him in glory.

Isn't this *also* a meaningful one? And doesn't it really belong more with *ye* than with *appear*? In this verse, a reader could emphasize *also*, along with *ye*.

again

In modern English, the word *again* means a second (or later) time. In the King James Version of the Bible, it doesn't necessarily have this meaning. Where it means a second time, it may require stress; in other cases, it probably does not.

Read this from Matthew 26:32:

> But after I am risen again, I will go before you into Galilee.

Here, *again* is used in the sense of back. Jesus did not rise from the dead twice. Hence, *again* should be subdued in this verse.

But consider this from John 4:11:

> Whosoever drinketh of this water shall thirst again.

In this verse, *again* does mean a second time and would be emphasized.

always, ever, never

Except where these words are in strong contrast, with each other, or with *sometimes*, occasions to emphasize them would be very infrequent.

In summary, words like these inherently carry with them enough emphasis, so additional emphasis by the reader is unnecessary.

22

Other Grammatical Constructions

Parenthetical expressions

A parenthetical expression is a part of a sentence which is separate from the main thought. In most cases it could be omitted without changing the grammatical structure of the sentence or its essential meaning. It could be as simple as a phrase or clause which modifies something in the sentence. Or it could be an abrupt interruption of the thought. Sometimes, the parenthetical expression is placed where the sentence flows easily with it. At other times, however, parenthetical expressions can be quite awkward to read. Despite the name parenthetical, these expressions are not always separated by parentheses, and need to be looked at carefully.

The listener needs to be able to tell when an expression is parenthetical in order to understand what the main verb in the sentence is, or what the subject is.

The reader can make these points clear by pausing before and/or after the expression, by lowering the pitch, or by both. Avoid a completely falling inflection at the end of the parenthetical expression, since the sentence is not complete at that point.

The phrasing of parenthetical expressions depends a great deal on the function of the expression in the sentence. Here briefly, are the different kinds of parenthetical expressions you may find.

- Nonrestrictive modifiers that don't end the sentence as in this from Chapter 15:

  My mother | who lives in Spokane | is coming to visit me.

- Parenthetical expressions that are similar to appositives. Appositives carry the same level of emphasis as the antecedent.

  I have made the earth, and created man upon it: I | even my hands | have stretched out the heavens, and all their host have I commanded. (Isaiah 45:12)

  In this verse, you would keep the same level of emphasis on the parenthetical, *even my hands,* with the stress on the word *my,* as on the word *I,* and would pause before and after the expression.

- Parenthetical expressions that are not part of the grammatical structure of the passage. These expressions could be omitted without changing or confusing the meaning, and are usually read as an aside in a lower pitch than the rest of the sentence.

  He was | I should say | about sixteen years old.

  We have found her to be | (and now I'm quoting your favorite author) | 'unlearned in the world's false subtleties.'

  He first findeth his own brother Simon, and saith unto him, We have found the Messias, which is | being interpreted | the Christ. (John 1:41)

  In this verse, *being interpreted* would be read in a lower pitch.

- Other parenthetical expressions that contain some new idea that requires emphasis.

> The public knew that it had in Lord Palmerstone not only a high-mettled master, but also a devoted servant—that he was, in every sense of the word, a public man. (Lytton Strachey, *Queen Victoria*)

Doesn't the parenthetical here "*in every sense of the word,*" present a new idea—the degree of his devotion—wouldn't you need to emphasize ***every sense***? You could make a slight pause either before or after the parenthetical expression.

> And forthwith Jesus gave them leave. And the unclean spirits went out, and entered into the swine: and the herd ran violently down a steep place into the sea, (they were about two thousand;) and were choked in the sea. (Mark 5:13)

In this verse, since the parenthetical gives new—and perhaps quite surprising—information about the swine—wouldn't you need a stress on **two thousand?** The phrase really goes with the mention of the swine, earlier in the verse, not with what immediately precedes it or follows it. So wouldn't you make a slight pause before and after the parenthetical?

Phrasal verbs

Phrasal verbs are verbs that have two or more words, the second being either an adverb or a preposition. For purposes of this discussion, we will call these second words *particles*. Phrasal verbs can be intransitive—without an object: *come in, watch out, rise up;* or transitive—with a direct object: *pour in the water, throw out those papers, put up the poster.*

> And the sons of the prophets were sitting before him: and he said unto his servant, Set on the great pot, and seethe pottage for the sons of the prophets. (II Kings 4: 38)

The verb *set on* is a phrasal verb. The verb is not *set*, followed by a prepositional phrase *on the great pot*! The servant was not told to do something **on** the pot, he was to do something **to** the pot—i.e., set the pot on the fire.

The emphasis for phrasal verbs follows the same principle of stressing the new idea or contrast and subduing the old idea. But when the **verb** is the new idea or contrast, the **particle** is stressed. Here are a few examples:

> The invitation said to come **in** at 6:00.
> Would you please throw **out** those papers?
> Gladys put **on** her new skirt.
> Nick and Cynthia made **up** a great story.
> The thieves held **up** the grocery store.

When there is a phrasal verb in a construction that is potential to actual, you would usually stress the verb in the second instance—the actual—as that presents a contrast.

> The invitation said to come **in** [potential], so we **came** in [actual].

> She asked me to throw **out** those papers [potential], so I **threw** out [actual] those papers.

In reading the Bible—particularly the King James Version—it is sometimes a challenge to differentiate between a phrasal verb and a regular verb with a prepositional phrase. In Proverbs 25:2 we read:

> It is the glory of God to conceal a thing: but the honour of kings is to search out a matter.

This verse has a phrasal verb: *search out*. The emphasis is on *out*.

Or consider Philippians 2: 12:

> Wherefore, my beloved, as ye have always obeyed, not as in my presence only, but now much more in my absence, work out your own salvation with fear and trembling.

The phrasal verb here is *work out* and the accent falls on *out*.

Is there a way to distinguish whether it is a verb phrase or a phrasal verb? Indeed there is. Replace what appears to be the direct object of the phrasal verb with a pronoun. Does it naturally fit between the verb and the particle?

> She asked me to throw out those papers. She said throw them out tomorrow.

> Gladys put on her new skirt. She put it on with her new sweater.

If so, you have a phrasal verb. With a phrasal verb, in conversation we put the accent on the particle and make a slight hesitation after the particle:

> If I say, I will forget my complaint, I will leave off my heaviness, and comfort myself: (Job 9:27)

Is *leave off* a phrasal verb? Try the test. Does it make sense to say leave it off? Yes, so treat *leave off* as a phrasal verb and emphasize *off* and make a slight pause after it.

> Then certain of the vagabond Jews, exorcists, took upon them to call over them which had evil spirits the name of the Lord Jesus, saying, we adjure you by Jesus whom Paul preacheth. (Acts 19:13)

Is the verb *call over*—as in, they called me over? Or, is it *call*, with the direct object being *the name of the Lord Jesus*? They are calling *the name of the Lord Jesus* over *them which had evil spirits*. Therefore, this is not a phrasal verb. In that case, you would make a light stress on *call,* followed by a slight pause, but there would be no stress on *over.* You would also want to make a slight pause after *spirits.*

23

Do we ever stress an old idea? Do we ever subdue a new idea?

When an old idea becomes new again; Newness due to intervening opposite

If a word is repeated after its opposite has been said, it has become new again. You re-stress the repeated word as a contrast.

If you say, "She wore a black hat and I'll wear a black hat," the second *black hat* is an old idea and would be subdued. But if you say "She wore a black hat and they wore white hats. I'll wear a black hat," you will stress *black* again. Even though it is appears to be an old idea, its opposite, white, has come in between. This makes the second *black* new, as a contrast to white.

Here is a Biblical example, from I John 2:16:

> For all that is in the world, the lust of the flesh, and the lust of the eyes, and the pride of life, is not of the Father, but is of the world.

At the end of the verse, *world* is an old idea, but because *the Father* has been introduced since *world* was last stated, you would stress the second *world* again, as a contrast.

Newness due to distance from the original word.

When the idea, or even the exact word, has been said so long before that the hearer has probably stopped thinking about it, you would re-stress it, as it becomes new again. An old idea does not stay old forever.

Newness of definition of a repeated word.

Sometimes a word may be repeated, but the definition of that word the second time may be different from the definition of the word as used the first time. When reading, you are looking for new and old ideas, not just new and old words. Consider I Peter 5:7:

> Casting all your care upon him; for he careth for you,

Readers often subdue *careth* because they have just read *care*. Sometimes, because they feel they have to have something to emphasize, they stress *you* or *he* or both, even though these are indisputably old ideas, echoing *your* and *him*. *Careth*, however, is an entirely different idea from *care*, because *care* means *burden* and *careth* means *looks after* (and in fact they are entirely different words in the original Greek). Therefore, you would consider *careth* a new idea, and you would stress it, subduing *you*.

Newness of tense

We have already seen examples of newness of tense in our discussion of Potential to Actual.

> Father, glorify thy name. Then came there a voice from heaven, saying, I have both glorified it, and will glorify it again. (John 12:28).

Both *glorified* and the final *glorify* are old. The newness here is the change of tense from *glorify* to *have glorified* and *will glorify*. *Have* and *will* bring out the contrast and are emphasized.

Newness of voice

> For now we see through a glass, darkly; but then face to face: now I know in part; but then shall I know even as also I am known (I Corinthians 13:12).

Almost without giving it a thought we stress *known*. Although *known* may appear to be an old idea, the newness lies in the voice, in the switch from active voice to passive.

> Be not overcome of evil, but overcome evil with good. (Romans 12:21)

The first *overcome* is in the passive voice; the second is in the active voice. So the second *overcome* is new and therefore to be emphasized.

No newness at all: complete restatement

Sometimes, as often in Psalms and Proverbs, the second half of a verse may be an exact restatement of the first. Each word in the second half may be a precise synonym of one in the first. What do you do? You can't subdue a whole clause; you can't mutter an entire half of a long verse under your breath. Examine the words closely to see whether one word (idea) might possibly be considered as a bit newer or a contrast; if so, you can stress that one. But sometimes you will find that the ideas in all the words are equally old. In this case, just read the second half as if it were the first thing you were reading. Consider it a chorus.

In Proverbs 2:3 we read:

> If thou criest after knowledge, and liftest up thy voice for understanding . . .

The words *liftest up thy voice for* have the same meaning as *criest after*; *thy* and *thou* refer to the same thing (the same idea); *knowledge* and *understanding* also are similar, but, since there is perhaps some very fine distinction between them, you might logically stress *understanding*. Others might consider the whole second half a word-for-word (idea by idea) repetition of the first half, as in Proverbs 4:14, where the entire second half is a precise restatement of the first half.

> Enter not into the path of the wicked, and go not in the way of evil men.

Go not in is substantially the same as *enter not into; the way of evil men* is the same as *the path of the wicked*. You cannot just mumble the whole second clause; so you must cast about for some word or words to lean on. Well, how would you say "go not in the way of evil men" if it opened the sentence? Probably you would stress *evil*. If so, stress *evil* when you read the entire verse.

Newness of relationship

Occasionally you will find a clause in which all the ideas have been presented but in which two of the repeated words, retaining their very same meanings, may have new positions in relation to each other, as in Genesis 32:

> [27] And he said unto him, What is thy name? And he said Jacob.
> [29] And Jacob asked him, and said, Tell me, I pray thee, thy name.

In verse 29, although *Jacob* and *him* are not new, their relationship to each other, their relative positions, are new. *Asking* is old, but the asked and the asker have changed places. The asker has become the asked, and the asked the asker. So you stress *Jacob* and *him*. You stress it as you would a sentence like "I helped **him** and **he** helped **me**."

Newness in the thought of the speaker

Sometimes, especially in the reading of direct conversation, we have to ask ourselves not what is the new idea in the **sentence**, but what is new in the thought of the **speaker** being quoted, or even what the speaker thinks is new in the thought of the **hearer** being addressed.

In the following reading of Isaiah 29 people sometimes think part of the way through the relationship of ideas and fail to go the final step.

> [11] And the vision of all is become unto you as the words of a book that is sealed, which men deliver to one that is learned saying, Read this, I pray thee: and he saith, I cannot; for it is sealed: [12] And the book is delivered to him that is not learned, saying, Read this, I pray thee: and he saith, I am not learned.

As a reader of verse 12 you might stress *he* and the second *I* and *learned*. But remember that "I am not learned" is direct conversation of the speaker "that is not learned". He doesn't know that you have just read about how somebody else said that he couldn't read the unsealed book; so he wouldn't stress *I* as a contrast to the former speaker. He would stress *learned*. However, you, the reader, could emphasize *he* in verse 12, because this is part of the narrative, contrasting it with the person who responded in verse 11.

> And the book is delivered to him that is **not** learned, saying, **Read** this, I pray thee: and **he** saith, "I am not **learned**."

Always watch this when you are reading a mixture of direct talking and narrative. Sometimes you are the narrator of "he said this and that." Other times you are taking the voice of the speakers in the narrative. The decision should be based on what will best bring out the meaning of the conversations being read. Sometimes you may decide to read the dialogue with the stress you would use if it were presented as indirect discourse.

Reiteration

Sometimes we stress a word which signifies an entirely old idea, merely to reiterate it. Suppose you have written in a speech, "We must preserve our national integrity. That's the only way we can prosper. That's the only way we can remain sound. That's the only way we can maintain the world's respect." At first glance it might seem logical to stress the new ideas, *remain sound* and *maintain the world's respect*, and to subdue *That's the only way* the second and third times it is said. It may well be more effective to keep driving home the same point by re-stressing *That's the only way* each time and placing a lighter or an equal stress on the new ideas. Isaiah 33:22 reads:

> For the Lord is our judge, the Lord is our lawgiver, the Lord is our king.

If this is your opening verse, you would probably emphasize the first *Lord*, and *judge*, *lawgiver*, and *king*, subduing the second and third *Lords* and all three *ours*. If, however, you have just been reading about false judges or other judges or kings, you may change your emphasis because of carry-over. You may stress the first *Lord* more heavily, but subdue *judge*, *lawgiver* and *king*, and re-stress the second and third *Lords*.

For the **Lord** is our judge, the **Lord** is our lawgiver the **Lord** is our king.

Subduing a New Idea

Just as we sometimes emphasize an old idea, so we sometimes subdue a new idea, or what may look like a new idea. Just as we can stress old ideas in Isaiah 33:22 for the purpose of reiteration, so we can subdue two new ideas: *lawgiver* and *king*.

24

Should We Read a Passage the Same Way Every Time?

Normally, once you think you have determined how a certain citation should be subdued and stressed, you will naturally stress it the same way each time. But often someone applying these principles will find that a sentence which has been almost always read in one certain way could also logically be stressed or phrased quite differently. Perhaps you may feel that this new reading, once discovered, is now the only logical way and that no carry-over would ever change it.

But don't just decide on one way to phrase and emphasize and then mechanically read the sentence that way every time. You are merely copying your own reading of the sentence instead of thinking of the meaning in a perhaps new context each time. You must think the meaning each time, just as if for the first time.

Then there are those who feel that a sentence should be read a different way each time. They feel that this preserves spontaneity. But ask yourself: Does the meaning change every time? Unless the meaning itself changes (and it may well do so, from carry-over), how can the emphasis change?, If you find a sentence in which the meaning never varies and if you conclude that there is just one way to bring out this meaning, why would you change your reading?

Someone may then protest, "But then everyone would read it exactly alike!" To which I always feel like replying, "So what! What's so awful about everyone bringing out the meaning?"

Tests for changing a reading

When you decide that logic requires a change from the usual phrasing or emphasis of a passage, you may be pleased with the new way, but if the changes are really drastic it is a good idea to put them to three tests.

1. Does it give a new meaning?
2. Does it clarify something usually not understood?
3. Is the clarification important enough to justify your listener's missing the next few sentences while they mull over the surprising new reading?
4. Will they get it? (The acid test.)

Some have said to me: "I know these changes in phrasing and emphasis are unusual and surprising, but, now that I've seen the new, sound meaning, I can't go back to the old way." If you are reasonably sure that your audience will grasp what your reading conveys, be sure it is true to the **writer's** meaning.

PART FIVE

More About
Common Denominator

25

Multiple Common Denominators

As we said in Chapter 10, Common Denominator Construction, the common denominator is always expressed twice. It is expressed by the same word(s) twice, or by a word(s) and a synonym or pronoun. To complete the construction, there are always two ideas about the cd that are in contrast with each other or at least in distinction or comparison.

Twiceness is the reason for the term *common denominator.* There have to be at least two things in order to have something in common. The denominator is what the two contrasts have in common.

A complete CD construction has the four essentials: two statements of the cd and two contrasts. But there are also multiple CD constructions: double, triple, quadruple and even more elaborate ones.

A triple CD construction contains three statements of the cd and three contrasts, as in the following sentence:

> His final will has provided affluence for his cousin, doled out a pittance to his sister, and left nothing to his brother.

Provided, doled out, and *left* are enough similar in meaning to constitute a triple denominator. You could switch these words and it would not change the meaning. *Affluence, pittance,* and *nothing* are three definite contrasts, each one contrasted with the others. This alone makes a complete triple CD construction. But there just happens to be another triple contrast, in *cousin, sister, and brother* the three beneficiaries. The triple-triple CD would therefore be read as follows:

> His final will has provided **affluence** for his **cousin**, doled out a **pittance** to his **sister**, and left **nothing** to his **brother**.

There is a triple CD construction in Hamlet's soliloquy, although many actors fail to realize this and therefore emphasize too many words. Can you remember how you have heard it?

> Whether 'tis nobler in the mind to suffer
> The slings and arrows of outrageous fortune,
> Or to take arms against a sea of troubles,
> And by opposing end them?

Aren't *the slings and arrows of outrageous fortune* and *a sea of troubles* talking about the same thing? And *them* repeats both. These are the three statements of the common denominator. *Suffer, take arms against* and *end* are the three contrasts, and would be stressed. (It would be conversational to stress only *arms* in *take arms against*).

It is such a famous quotation that it is hard to resist the temptation to punch the words you have always heard jabbed. But we have seen that *slings and arrows of outrageous fortune, a sea of troubles,* and *them* are your triple cd; so they should be subdued. The whole sentence swings on the contrasting *suffer, take arms against*, and *end.*

Substitution

When the second statement of the common denominator is a synonym of the first statement you can use either statement both times.

Let's try using one wording of the cd idea three times. Let's start with sea of troubles:

Whether 'tis nobler in the mind to **suffer**
A sea of troubles
Or to take up **arms** against a sea of troubles,
And by opposing **end** a sea of troubles?

It makes sense, doesn't it? Now let's use the *slings and arrows of outrageous fortunes*:

Whether 'tis nobler in the mind to **suffer**
The slings and arrows of outrageous fortune
Or to take up **arms** against
The slings and arrows of outrageous fortune,
And by opposing **end**
The slings and arrows of outrageous fortune

Using the same **words** to express the cd—the **idea** that is the same—makes the contrast clear and naturally emphasized.

Another way to illustrate multiple cd's is by using pronouns in place of the cd statement. If we are thinking beforehand about the slings and arrows of outrageous fortune, we might say:

Whether 'tis nobler to **suffer** them,
Or to take up **arms** against them,
And by opposing **end** them.

Switchability

Another way to verify cd's is when you can switch the terms that express the cd without changing the meaning.

Whether 'tis nobler in the mind to **suffer**
A sea of troubles
Or to take up **arms** against them,
And by opposing **end** the slings and arrows of outrageous fortune?

Consider I Peter 4:10:

As every man hath received the gift, even so minister the same one to another as good stewards of the manifold grace of God.

What is *the gift?* Isn't it *the manifold grace of God?* And certainly *the same* must stand for something that went before. Isn't it also referring to *the gift?* Isn't that idea the common denominator? Try reading the verse substituting *the gift* for *the same* and for *the manifold grace of God?* Then try using the words *manifold grace of God* each time?

As every man hath **received** the gift, even so **minister** the gift one to another, as good **stewards** of the gift.

As every man hath **received** the manifold grace of God, even so **minister** the manifold grace of God one to another, as good **stewards** of the manifold grace of God.

You could also switch *the gift* and *the manifold grace of God.*

As every man hath **received** the manifold grace of God, even so **minister the** same one to another, as good **stewards** of the gift.

I've gone into all this not just because it's fun to experiment with switching in a switchable CD construction but also because I want you to play this little game yourself. Playing this little game will give you a **feeling** for CD and make you **think** in CD.

Recap

When the cd is expressed in different words rather than in identical words, you can:

- Use either expression both times.
- Switch the expressions.
- Restate the sentence using pronouns for both or all the cd expressions.

PRACTICE EXAMPLES

1. A word is dead when it is said, some say. I say it just begins to live that day. (Emily Dickinson)
2. If ye, then being evil, know how to give good gifts to your children, how much more shall your Father which is in heaven give good things to them that ask him? (Matthew 7:11)
3. The course you recommend leads to progress, but the policy he sanctions leads to disaster.

DISCUSSION

1. The contrasts are clear here: *dead* with *live* and *some* with *I*. What are the common denominators? Doesn't *that day* at the end of the second sentence mean the same thing as *when it is said*? Doesn't the pronoun *it* mean *word*, the same idea expressed three times? And isn't *say*, expressed twice, another common denominator? So the only words that need emphasis are the contrasts, *dead*, *some I* and *live*. All the words that express the common denominator ideas should be subdued

2. Isn't *give good things* the same idea as *give good gifts?* That's a common denominator, and the words that express it would be subdued. What are the contrasts? Aren't ***ye*** and ***evil*** in contrast to ***Father*** and ***heaven?*** Those two sets of contrasts refer to the one cd. Is there another cd in this verse? Is *them that ask* the same as *children?* The contrasts are ***your*** (those that ask **you**) and ***him*** (**his**) children.

3. The contrast between *disaster* and *progress* is clear, those words would be stressed. Their common denominator is the idea *leads to,* stated in the same words, and therefore subdued each time. Is there another common denominator here? Isn't *sanctions* similar to *recommend?* And isn't *policy* the same as *course?* These two common denominators share one pair of contrasts—*you* and *he*. The statements of each common denominator would be subdued, only the contrasts would be stressed, so you would only stress four words in this sentence: *you, progress, he disaster*, making the meaning clear from the outset.

26

Analogies

An analogy is a sentence in which something unknown or unfamiliar is explained by likening it to something familiar. A very simple analogy is found in Psalm 125:2:

> As the mountains are round about Jerusalem, so the Lord is round about his people.

This verse contains a complete CD construction, with two sets of contrasts. The cd is *are round about* and *is round about. Lord* is contrasted with *mountains*, and *people* is contrasted with *Jerusalem.* All you need to emphasize are the contrasts, *mountains, Jerusalem, Lord,* and *people.*

The words *as* and *so* used here will alert you to an analogy, but not all analogies are as easy to recognize and to read aloud. The easiest way to figure out the reading of an analogy is just to tell yourself: All right, here's another CD construction. So I'll read it that way.

One great writer closely associated with analogies was Homer. His writing is full of majestic comparisons called Homeric similes. Here is the Long, Leaf and Myers translation from the *Illiad:*

> And even as the goatherds easily divide the ranging flocks of goats when they mingle in the pasture, so did their captains marshal them [his men] on this side and on that, to enter into the fray.

This array of poetic words may look forbidding at the first glance, but we are concerned primarily with only four of them: *goatherds, goats, captains, them.* We find also our old friends *as* and *so*.

Isn't *captains* compared with *goatherds*, and isn't *them* [his men] compared with *goats*? So we have two sets of comparisons. Then what are the cd words?

As the goatherds [do something] to the goats
So their captains [do something] to them.

Aren't *divide* and *marshal* enough alike to qualify as the common denominator?

As the **goatherds** divide the **goats**
So their **captains** did marshal **them.**

Divide and *marshal* being the two statements of the cd, they are subdued.

[If you also caught the contrast between *mingle in the **pasture*** and *enter into the **fray***, congratulations. You have become an analytical reader.

In this next example the analogy is reversed - the known or familiar thing is stated last. However, the analysis is the same.

For the ear trieth words as the mouth tasteth meat. (Job 34:3)

Aren't *tasteth* and *trieth* the common denominator here? Those words would be subdued. And the contrasts would be *ear* contrasted with *mouth* and *words* contrasted with *meat*, so those four words would be stressed.

For the **ear** trieth **words** as the **mouth** tasteth **meat.**

PRACTICE EXAMPLES

1. As a hart longs for flowing streams, so longs my soul for thee, O God. (Psalm 42:1 Revised Standard Version)

2. For as by one man's disobedience many were made sinners, so by the obedience of one shall many be made righteous. (Romans 5:19)

3. For as the earth bringeth forth her bud, and as the garden causeth the things that are sown in it to spring forth; so the Lord God will cause righteousness and praise to spring forth before all the nations. (Isaiah 61:11)

4. We all know, that as the human body can be nourished on any food, though it were boiled grass and the broth of shoes, so the human mind can be fed by any knowledge. (Ralph Waldo Emerson, *The American Scholar*)

DISCUSSION

1. The common denominator here is stated twice: *longs for.* The two sets of contrast/comparison are *hart* with *soul,* and *streams* with *thee.* Those are the only words that would be stressed.

2. It's easiest to start looking for the contrasts here: what is *disobedience* contrasted with? *Obedience.* What is *sinners* contrasted with? *Righteous.* Those are the words to stress. Isn't *one man's* the same idea as *of one?* That is one idea that is a cd. And isn't *many were made* and *shall many be made* the same idea? That is the second cd. As **dis**obedience is to **sinners** so **obedience** is to **righteous.** These contrast words are all that need to be emphasized.

3. The idea that is the common denominator is expressed three times in this verse. There are two examples from nature, two things that are known, used to explain one metaphysical action. This common denominator is expressed once as *bringeth forth* and twice as *spring forth.* One set of contrasts is *earth, garden* and *Lord God.* The second set is *bud, things that are sown,* and *righteousness and praise.* In the phrase *things that are sown,* the modifier carries the meaning, so you would only need to stress *sown.* As the **earth** is to the **bud** and the **garden** is to what is **sown** in it, so the **Lord God** is to **righteousness** and **praise.**

4. *Human can be nourished* and *human can be fed* are the words that express the common denominator. The contrasts are ***body*** with ***mind*** and ***food*** with ***knowledge.***

27

Incomplete Common Denominator Constructions

Three-quarter CD constructions

There is a CD construction where one or more of the common denominators is omitted and merely implied. Sometimes it is the first denominator which is omitted; sometimes it is the second. Let's start with the following:

Her cause for rejoicing was also her **father's** cause for rejoicing.

Cause for rejoicing is the cd, expressed twice. The first *her* and *father's* are the two contrasts. But you could state the thought just as clearly if you said:

Her cause for rejoicing was also her **father's**.

This time instead of the denominator being stated twice, it is stated only once—but **implied** a second time. We call this a three-quarter CD construction since one quarter of the construction is missing. But it is a CD construction all the same with the two contrast words stressed.

Here is another three-quarter CD construction:

His **eyes**, not his **words**, revealed his true feelings.

Clearly, *eyes* and *words* are the two contrast words, and *revealed his true feelings* is the cd, expressed only once. Filled out, this would read:

His **eyes** revealed his true feeling—not his **words** revealed his true feelings.

From Chief Justice Earl Warren:

It is the spirit not the form of law that keeps justice alive.

Isn't the idea "of law" clearly implied after the word *spirit?* So *of law* is the cd. The contrast would be between *spirit* and *form*. You need to subdue "of law" so that the implied contrast is clearly stated.

In this example from Andrew Jackson, (Library of Congress) the singly stated cd—*interest of the country*—comes between the two contrasts.

The **agricultural** interest of the country is connected with every **other**, and superior in importance to them all.

How would you read what Hamlet says to Guildenstern?

You would sound me from my lowest note to the top of my compass.

Did you stress *lowest, note, top,* and *compass*? But if you filled out the CD construction, wouldn't it be *note of my compass* and *top note*? Then you would subdue *note* and *of my compass* and contrast *lowest* with *top*.

You would sound me from the **lowest** note [of my compass] to the **top** [note] of my compass.

One-half CD constructions

Sometimes you will uncover a half CD construction. Let's examine this sentence:

Let Agnes attend to it.

If you stressed *Agnes* and *attend,* you are saying that whatever "it" is will be taken care of by Agnes and not ignored. But if you stress *Agnes* and subdue *attend to it,* you now have a half-CD construction and therefore an entirely different meaning. *Agnes* is the contrast (implied) and *attend to it* is the cd. You have implied something like:

Let **Agnes** attend to it but do not let **Dora** attend to it.

This is your full CD construction, with *Dora* as the other contrast word, and the second *attend to it* as the second statement of the cd. If you say "Let **Agnes** attend to it," you have made a half-CD construction, obviously implying a contrast between Agnes and anyone other than Agnes.

A half-CD construction may also consist of only two words, as:

Agnes went.

This is also perfectly logical. *Agnes* is contrasted with implied somebody or nobody else.

Agnes ***went.***

This would imply that Agnes did not remain. She went.

Essential facts about Common Denominator

1. The common denominator (the cd) is an old idea in the thought of the writer and therefore old in the thought of the speaker at the outset.

2. The word or words expressing the cd are subdued.

3. A complete CD construction contains four parts: two statements or expressions of the cd and two contrasts.

4. There is always at least a twiceness to other CD constructions as well. In a full CD construction the cd is expressed twice. In a ¾ CD construction the cd is expressed once and clearly implied a second time.

5. There are always at least two ideas saying something about the common denominator. These are the contrasts.

6. The contrast words are stressed.

7. A CD construction may contain three statements of the cd and three contrasts, or an unlimited number of them.

8. The presence of two synonymous ideas or two contrasting ideas does not necessarily mean that the sentence contains a common denominator. All four parts must be present in a complete CD construction.

9. A CD construction is usually found within a single sentence but can spread over more if the sentences are so clearly related in thought that they could easily be connected as one.

10. When a reader or an actor subdues the cd statement or statements, the idea that is the cd instantly becomes old in the thought of the hearer, and the hearer gets the message.

PRACTICE EXAMPLES

1. Welcome the coming, speed the parting guest. (Alexander Pope)

2. Blessed art thou, Simon Bar-jonah, for flesh and blood hath not revealed it unto thee, but my Father which is in heaven. (Matthew 16;17)

3. For I am not come to call the righteous, but sinners to repentance. (Matthew 9:13)

4. And if the blind lead the blind, both shall fall into the ditch. (Matthew 15:14)

DISCUSSION

1. There are two sets of obvious contrasts here: *welcome/speed* and *coming/parting.* Isn't *guest* implied after *coming?* Welcome the coming what? So *guest* is the common denominator, implied once, stated once, and it should be subdued. All four contrast words need to be stressed to make the meaning clear: ***welcome, coming, speed, parting.***

2. What is *my Father which is in heaven* in contrast with? Isn't it *flesh and blood?* Is there a common denominator? Isn't *hath revealed it unto thee* implied at the end of the verse – doesn't this make sense? My Father which is in heaven hath revealed it unto thee. The common denominator is *hath revealed it unto thee*, expressed once and implied a second time. So we subdue the phrase that expresses the common denominator, and stress only the words that bring out the contrasts: *blood, Father, heaven.*

3. Is *to repentance* a new idea at the end of the verse? Or is it implied after *the righteous?* "I am not come to call the righteous to repentance..." Isn't it a common denominator, implied once and stated once? It should be subdued and only the words that bring out the contrast should be stressed: *righteous, sinners.*

4. Is there an implied contrast here in the first half of the sentence? What would the contrast be—with the blind leading the seeing? With the blind doing something else to

the blind? Or with the seeing leading the blind? The idea of leading the blind is the common denominator. In this half-Common Denominator construction, the contrast and the cd are stated only once, but the implied contrast is clear if you emphasize the first *blind* and subdue *lead the blind.*

28

First-timeness

There is one outstanding characteristic of the actor who reads lines naturally or the announcer who reads a radio script as if he were just talking. That is what has been called "first-time-ness." This means the quality of sounding as if you were saying the words for the first time, as if a new thought just came to you as you were speaking. It is the opposite of the principle behind common denominator, when there is already something on the speaker's mind. Consider this sentence:

> Some people bring happiness wherever they go, some whenever they go.

You might see right away that there is a contrast between *where* and *when*, and a common denominator—*people bring happiness* and *they go.* But if you read the sentence, subduing the common denominator words and just stressing the contrasts, you would lose the surprise, and the joke would fall pretty flat.

Reading for first timeness, you want your listener to be surprised, to not know where you are going. So you would want to read this sentence emphasizing the new ideas *bring happiness* and *go* in the first half of the sentence, and **not** stressing the first contrast, *where.* Then, after a slight pause, stress only the contrast, *when,* in the second half.

> Some people bring **happiness** wherever they **go** | some **when**ever they go.

Common Denominator is substantially the opposite of first-timeness, and usually immeasurably more significant. In reading for first-timeness you sound as if you have not planned the whole sentence. You do not know what you are going to say next. CD, however, indicates what you are thinking, that you have planned what you are going to say next, and the hearer thinks ahead with you. When CD is used, the hearer, like the speaker, actor, or reader, knows the end from the beginning. When first-timeness is used it brings out a spontaneity, a surprise for the listener.

When CD is not used the hearer does not know what is coming next. Take this line from Fred Astaire:

> The hardest job kids face today is learning good manners without seeing any.

Do you see a Common Denominator construction here? Doesn't the pronoun *any* stand for *good manners?* And isn't there a contrast between *learning* and *seeing*? But if you read this sentence stressing just the contrast in the first half, your listener knows what's coming, and you've lost the surprise and the humor. Isn't it more spontaneous to use first timeness and treat the first half of the sentence as though these are all new ideas, as you don't know what's coming? Many a quip is ruined because a speaker does not know how to guard his punches by disguising his lines with first-timeness. The story teller often needs to avoid CD, so as to give his hearers a surprise at the end. You must make your audience feel that each idea, each phrase, is coming to you just at the moment you utter it.

The use of first-timeness isn't just to surprise. It can be used to show a stream of consciousness on the part of the speaker; some new truth coming to the speaker, as in this quote from Ralph Waldo Emerson.

Some books leave us free. Some books **make** us free.

You have choices

Be ye therefore merciful, as your Father also is merciful. (Luke 6:36)

Without looking past the first *merciful*, wouldn't you stress merciful as a new idea, then go on to contrast *Father* with (the unstressed) *ye* and to subdue the second *merciful*? That would be first-timeness.

Be ye therefore **merciful,** as your **Father also** is merciful.

But another reader might prefer CD, subduing each *merciful* and stressing *ye* and *Father*. [**You** be that way, as your **Father** is that way.] In this way of reading it, the contrast is pre-thought-out. You were reading the sentence as if your whole purpose in reading it—in saying it—were just to make the contrast. It is no news that somebody is to be merciful; you take that for granted, and your point is to parallel **your** being merciful with your **Father** being merciful.

Be **ye** therefore merciful, as your **Father also** is merciful.

You have this choice again in John 15:12:

That ye love one another, as I have loved you.

First-timeness would stress *love* and subdue *ye* and *one another*. CD would subdue *love*, stressing *ye* in contrast to *I*, and *another* in contrast to *you*.

First-timeness:
That ye **love** one another, as **I** have loved **you.**

Common Denominator construction:
That **ye** love one **another,** as **I** have loved **you.**

There are times when first-timeness will lend a conversational tone and be the most effective reading. However, First-timeness is a grace note. Common Denominator is a resounding chord.

PART SIX

More About Phrasing

29

Interrupted Speeches

One of the most difficult things for an actor or a reader to handle effectively is an interrupted speech—a speech broken off by someone else or by oneself.

> *The Queen turned crimson with fury, and, after glancing at her for a moment like a wild beast, screamed, "Off with her head! Off—"*
>
> *"Nonsense!" said Alice, very loudly and decidedly, and the Queen was silent.*
>
> Lewis Carroll: *Alice's Adventures in Wonderland.*

Suppose these quotations are the lines of a play and you are playing the part of the Queen. You want to sound as if you are really interrupted on the second *off* and you want to sound as if you didn't know you were going to be interrupted. The worst way to read the line, by emphasizing and holding the last word, indicates clearly that you know the other actor is supposed to interrupt you and you are just waiting for him to do so.

The key to a clear reading is to figure out what the whole speech would be if it were completed. Then actually start to say the whole thing and, when the other actor cuts you off, you will sound natural because you will actually **be** interrupted. The whole speech here would obviously have been "Off with her head!" and so you start to say the whole thing.

Now suppose that you are giving a reading of the whole play yourself and you have to impersonate both the Queen and Alice. This is much more difficult, of course. You have to interrupt **yourself.** The only way to do it convincingly is to imagine you are going to complete the sentence. This will help you to start the "Off—" with no more emphasis than you should use and to let go of it quickly by shouting with a different type of voice, "Nonsense!"

The opposite of a quick cutoff is the hesitation or stammer. Try reading this sentence: "I can't describe it exactly but it's—it's—well, it's—like a—a sudden plunge into icy water." The amateurish way to read it would be to stress and hold on to each *it's* and each *a* and—still worse—to pronounce each *a* as long a. (The indefinite article, unless stressed, is simply *uh.*) Imagine that you say the sentence without breaks, "I can't describe it exactly but it's like a sudden plunge into icy water." Then interrupt yourself on the first *it's,* making it staccato. The same holds true for the rest of the sentence: imagine at each break, that you are going to complete the sentence, then interrupt yourself. This is a feat of self-deception equal to the White Queen's cultivated ability to believe as many as six impossible things before breakfast. But with practice you can, like the white Queen, get the knack of it.

30

Finding Two Ideas Instead of Only One

Sometimes you run across a sentence that is usually read in a lump conveying just one idea, but which really has two or more important ideas which can be brought out if the reader sees them and if he knows how to make them stand out. Genesis 1:26 reads:

> And God said, Let us make man in our image, after our likeness.

Usually the reader is so intent on the idea of *in our image* that he misses the opportunity of bringing out something important: that after creating everything else, now God creates man. Isn't that a very new idea? So you would want a stress on man then a full stop, with a falling inflection. Let that idea "sink in" and then get to the next big idea of how God created man, stressing *image* and *likeness.*

Instead of focusing attention upon the sentence as a whole and especially on the last part, you let your listeners receive the idea in the first part and get the good out of it and then add the other idea.

Form the habit of analyzing your sentences to see whether they are constructed in this way. But don't make a mannerism of reading them like this. Use this trick of phrasing only when two ideas are really worth bringing out separately, or it will lose its effect and your reading will become monotonous.

> And they did all eat, and were filled: and they took up of the broken meat that was left seven baskets full. (Matthew 15:37)

This construction is similar. Can you see where you might give two ideas? Here, too, a key idea is neglected by not pausing before the last word. Often it is read with no pause at all between *baskets* and *full,* as though it were seven basketfuls. But there is a difference between a basketful and a basket full or a full basket. The point here is that there was enough left over to fill seven baskets, and that the baskets were full. This idea is given out by pausing after *baskets* and stressing *full.*

> And the Lord went before them by day in a pillar of a cloud, to lead them in the way; and by night in a pillar of fire. (Exodus 13:21)

If you pause after the first *them* long enough to focus attention on the idea of the Lord's going before them, you give your hearers one helpful idea to think about. Then you add another: the manner in which the Lord went before them by day and the manner by night. As this is frequently read, with no pause after the first *them,* the reader is rushing on to tell about the cloud and the fire and gives the listener no time to ponder the first helpful idea. The listener might just as well be allowed to savour two helpful thoughts instead of one, since they are both undeniably present in the text.

> And Abel, he also brought of the firstlings of his flock and of the fat thereof. (Genesis 4:4)

Sometimes you will find passages where two ideas ought to be given instead of just one, otherwise the meaning will be changed. In Genesis 4:4 there is usually no pause made after *brought.* This implies an illogical meaning. If you say without pause that "Abel also brought of the firstlings of his flock," you imply that Cain, (who had brought the fruit of the ground) too, had "brought of the firstlings of his flock." But the *also* goes with *brought* only, not with the whole expression. Therefore, you need to make a separation after *brought.* What Abel also did was to bring. He did not "also bring of the firstlings of his flock." So a definite pause after *brought*, together with a falling inflection, establishes the idea. Then you add the contrasting idea that what he brought was "of the firstlings of his flock."

The listener is allowed to savour two thoughts instead of one.

Overuse of this idea can result in something much worse than merely an annoying mannerism. It can produce personal misinterpretation. Both Moffatt's translation and the Greek text show that it would be definitely wrong to stop after *me* in the second verse of Romans 8.

> For the law of the Spirit of life in Christ Jesus hath made me free from the law of sin and death.

Don't attempt to establish the idea that the law has **made** me (created me), and then add a second idea, that it has not only created me but created me free. The verb is not *to make;* it is *to make free* or *to free.* So the only logical way to read this is the usual way of reading *made me free* with no pause between *me* and *free.*

PRACTICE EXAMPLES

1. And Peter went out, and wept bitterly. (Luke 22:62)
2. And the son said unto him, Father I have sinned against heaven, and in thy sight. . . . (Luke 15:21)

DISCUSSION

1. Isn't it news that Peter went out and wept? This isn't comparing weeping one way with another way, is it? Aren't each of these ideas—*wept* and *bitterly*—full of meaning here? Wouldn't you want to pause after *wept?* And use a falling inflection?

2. The son is telling his father that he has sinned. Isn't that a new idea? That is his confession. Then he amplifies that idea by stating that it is not only against God, but also against his father. So wouldn't you want a good pause after *sinned* with a falling inflection, and then a slight pause after *heaven*, but with a slightly rising inflection. You are not adding anything to the text here, you are just bringing out each new idea that the writer has put in.

31

Two Ideas in Conjunction

Though a sinner do evil an hundred times, and his days be prolonged, yet surely I know that it shall be well with them that fear God, which fear before him.
Ecclesiastes 8:12

This verse does not mean: I know it shall be well with them that fear God, though a sinner do evil an hundred times. Nor: I know that it shall be well with them that fear God, though a sinner's days be prolonged. The fact that a sinner does wrong is not especially disturbing and the fact that someone's days are prolonged is not disturbing. It is when the two things happen together that we might be disturbed; when a sinner does evil an hundred times and still his days are prolonged. Therefore, do not separate the two ideas by pausing after *times*. Read it almost as one idea, with no definite pause until after *prolonged.*

PRACTICE EXAMPLES

1. Then came Peter to him, and said, Lord, how oft shall my brother sin against me, and I forgive him? (Matthew 18:22)
2. [34] Come ye blessed of my Father, inherit the kingdom. . . . [35] For I was an hungered, and ye gave me meat: I was thirsty, and ye gave me drink: I was a stranger, and ye took

me in: [36] Naked, and ye clothed me: I was sick, and ye visited me: I was in prison, and ye came unto me. (Matthew 25)

3. They shall not build, and another inhabit; they shall not plant, and another eat: (Isaiah 65:22)

DISCUSSION

1. Is Peter asking Jesus how often his brother will sin? That is not the complete question here, is it? These are two independent clauses, with subject and verb, but the first one does not make the entire point alone. Aren't these two ideas connected into one question? So you wouldn't pause after *sin against me.*

2. Are these people being blessed because Jesus was hungry? No, it was because **when** he was hungry they gave him meat. In all the instances in this passage, it is the two ideas together—Jesus' condition and their response, that make the complete thought. So, although a comma separates them each time, don't you need to connect each time: after *hungered, thirsty, stranger, naked, sick* and *prison.*

3. Is the writer saying that the people shall not build? Does that make sense by itself? No. Doesn't it imply **When** they do build, no one else will inhabit. Aren't these two ideas in close conjunction? The first does not make sense by itself. So don't you need to be sure to connect and use a rising inflection after *build* and *plant?*

32

Connecting Word Followed by a Parenthetical Expression

Radio and television newscasters are usually reading from a script rather than speaking spontaneously. One way you can tell they are reading from a printed page is how they emphasize the connecting word that precedes a parenthetical expression set off by commas. This description sounds a little formidable but it is easy to recognize this construction.

We feel that, in the event of new developments, she should be notified.

That is the connecting word, followed by the parenthetical expression, *in the event of new developments,* set off by commas.

Because most people treat a comma as a red light, they pause after *that* and after *developments.* And because most untrained line-readers seem unable to pause without emphasizing or holding the word immediately preceding the pause, they stress *that* and *developments.*

It is all right to stress *developments,* because it is a new idea. But to stress *that* produces a very unnatural reading. You would not stress it when spontaneously talking, *that* being merely a connecting word with little or no meaning. You could even leave it out completely.

We feel in the event of new developments she should be notified.

Therefore, you subdue the word *that* so that it becomes merely *th't* (not *thut*), and then you should make no pause between *that* and *in*, even though there is a comma between them.

> We feel th't in the event of new developments, she should be notified.

When reading a sentence containing a connecting word followed by a parenthetical expression set off by commas, subdue the connecting word and do not pause after it. In conversation we almost never hear anyone pause after the connecting word, whether it is followed by a parenthetical expression or followed directly by the grammatical group it introduces.

> We feel that she should be notified.

It can be helpful to make a slight pause **before** the connecting word. That will help you make the connection after it.

> We feel | that in the event of new developments **|** she should be notified.

The word *that* is not the only connecting word to watch out for. Other connecting words (conjunctions and relative pronouns) are: *if, when, while, where, who, which, because, as, since, for, although, lest, inasmuch as.*

Try reading these familiar lines without stressing the connecting word and without pausing before the parenthetical expression (set off by commas).

Consider this verse from Ecclesiastes 3:14:

> I know that, whatsoever God doeth, it shall be forever.

Or from Mark 4:31:

It is like a grain of mustard seed, which, when it is sown in the earth, is less than all the seeds that be in the earth:

Or from the first line of the Declaration of Independence:

When, in the Course of human events, it becomes necessary for one people. . . .

Two from Carroll, *Alice's Adventures in Wonderland:*

For, with all her knowledge of history, Alice had no very clear notion how long ago anything happened.

The dormouse had closed its eyes by this time, and was going off into a doze; but, on being pinched by the Hatter, it woke up again. . . .

From the local news:

There were many people who, when asked, agreed to sign the petition.

Or from your mother:

It would help if, just once, you took your shoes off before walking on the carpet.

Now, when you read these sentences following this pattern, doesn't the reading sound completely natural?

33

Vocatives

Nobody would ever think of saying, "Come in | Louise, and-sit down," as it is natural to say, "Come in Louise | and sit down." You would naturally connect *Louise* with *Come in* and would pause after *Louise,* if at all. This would be done whether or not you had ever heard of what is called a vocative.

The vocative is the case of address. It is the name or the title of the person or thing you are speaking to, like *Louise* in the sentence above, or *pretty maiden* in "Tell me, pretty maiden, are there any more at home like you?" or *door* in "Now stay open, door, and don't bang shut again!"

For some reason, in spontaneous talking we almost always connect the vocative with what precedes and not with what follows. Listen to the talk around you and you will see that this is the way people phrase unconsciously when they use vocatives. The habit is so ingrained that almost anyone would automatically use this phrasing in reading aloud the sentences quoted above.

You usually wouldn't stress the vocative, as it is old in the thought of the speaker, since he would certainly know who he is talking to. However, if there is more than one vocative, if the speaker is speaking to more than one person or group, you might stress the second vocative as a contrast.

As in Deuteronomy 32:1:

Give **ear**, O ye heavens, and I will **speak;** and hear, O **earth,** the words of my mouth.

In addition to the emphasis and phrasing, the vocative usually takes a slightly rising inflection, especially when it comes in the middle of a sentence as in Psalm 21:13:

Be thou exalted, Lord, in thine own strength

However, if the speaker is calling the person to get his or her attention, the vocative will take a falling inflection and be emphasized:

Susan, watch out! It's icy!

PRACTICE EXAMPLES

1. Can the fig tree, my brethren, bear olive branches? (Isaiah 3:12)
2. Hear, ye children, the instruction of a father. . . . (Proverbs 4:1)
3. Search me, O God, and know my heart: (Psalm 139:23)
4. And Peter answered and said to Jesus, Master, it is good for us to be here. (Mark 9:5)
5. And he was in the hinder part of the ship, asleep on a pillow: and they awake him, and say unto him, Master, carest thou not that we perish? (Mark 4:38)

DISCUSSION

1. The vocative, *my brethren,* would be connected to what precedes it, *fig tree*. The vocative would not need a stress, but

you would use a slight rising inflection on *brethren* and a short pause after *brethren.*

2. Connect the vocative, *ye children,* to what precedes it, *Hear;* slight pause after *children* and rising inflection.

3. The vocative, *O God,* would go with what precedes it, and it is crucial to have the rising inflection at the end of the vocative. If you use a falling inflection on *O God* it can almost sound like an expletive—O God!

4. In this case the vocative *Master* is the start of Peter's quotation, so you can't really put it with what precedes it. It still doesn't need any stress. Just make a slight pause after *Master* and use a rising inflection.

5. In this instance, the disciples are not just having a conversation with Jesus, they are calling out to him, trying to wake him, so the vocative, *Master,* would be stressed and you would use a falling inflection.

34

Quotations

Don't let anyone persuade you that you are supposed to pause every time you see a quotation mark. You don't have to signal to your hearers that a quotation is coming or has just ended. When reading you should be thinking about the sense, not about the punctuation, as you do not think in terms of punctuation marks when you are just talking. You are trying to make your listeners feel spoken to, instead of read to.

Suppose you should run across a sentence like this:

> In giving them shelter you were hosts to "angels unawares."

Would you stop before *angels* as though you were announcing: "Quotation marks are coming!" Think of the sense and not of the punctuation. The quotation in this sentence comes from Hebrews 13:2.

> Thereby some have entertained angels unawares.

What does *unawares* go with? Is it the *angels* who are unawares or are the *some* (the people) entertaining them unawares? Isn't it the latter? So in reading this verse in Hebrews, don't you need to pause between *angels* and *unawares?*

When these two words—*angels unawares*—occur together as a quotation, as in the first sample sentence above, you have to ask the same question: What does *unawares* go with? It doesn't mean that you were hosts to **angels** that were unawares.

It means that **you** were hosting them unawares. Therefore, do not pause before the two quoted words and then read them as though they were one word. If there were no quotation marks there and you had never heard the quotation, you would naturally read it with no pause between *to* and *angels;* and to bring out the logical meaning, you would definitely pause between *angels* and *unawares* .

The main principle to apply when reading quotations is the principle of association: What Does it Modify or Belong With. Keep in mind what we have said earlier: The punctuation does not necessarily determine the phrasing.

The King James Version of the Bible does not use quotation marks, which can make it difficult for a reader to know how to phrase quotations. It may be helpful for the reader to write in light quotation marks in his Bible, so that he can see where the quotations begin and end.

Consider Luke 7:

> [40] And Jesus answering said unto him, Simon, I have somewhat to say unto thee. And he saith, Master, say on. [41] There was a certain creditor which had two debtors: the one owed five hundred pence, and the other fifty.

Who said "Master, say on"? Wasn't it Simon? But who said, "There was a certain creditor. . . ."? That was Jesus. So what you have here is two quotations from two different speakers, without any word indicating a change of speaker. What the reader can do here is to make an extra-long pause after "say on."

Or Luke 7:16:

> And there came a fear on all: and they glorified God, saying, That a great prophet is risen up among us; and, That God hath visited his people.

Unlike the previous example, this verse doesn't have a direct quotation. It has two indirect quotations, each beginning with the word *that*. Again, apply the principle What Does it Modify or Belong With. In this verse, what does *saying* belong with? Doesn't it belong more with what follows it? So you pause after *God* and connect after *saying*. Then pause after *among us*, to separate the two quotations. And you make no pause after the last *and*.

> And there came a fear on all: and they glorified God,|
> saying,_That a great prophet is risen up among us; |
> and_That God hath visited his people.

The word *saying* occurs frequently in the Bible, and nearly always you will find that it belongs more with what follows than with what precedes.

Consider Acts 17:18:

> Then certain philosophers of the Epicureans, and of the Stoicks, encountered him. And some said, What will this babbler say? other some, He seemeth to be a setter forth of strange gods: because he preached unto them Jesus and the resurrection.

In this verse, the reader will find it helpful to insert quotation marks. You would then come up with:

> Then certain philosophers of the Epicureans, and of the Stoicks, encountered him. And some said, "What will this babbler say?" other some, "He seemeth to be a setter forth of strange gods": because he preached unto them Jesus and the resurrection.

In this verse, it's important to understand that there are two quotations, and that the second quotation ends after *gods.* (You can confirm this by checking a modern translation, such as the New Revised Standard Version.) So the Reader needs to make it clear that the last part of the verse is not part of the quotation. He does this by making a long pause after *gods*.

And II Timothy 2: 19:

> Nevertheless the foundation of God standeth sure, having this seal, The Lord knoweth them that are his. And, Let every one that nameth the name of Christ depart from iniquity.

Again, you will have to consult a modern translation to understand where the quotations end. If you insert quotation marks, you will have:

> Nevertheless the foundation of God standeth sure, having this seal, "The Lord knoweth them that are his." And, "Let every one that nameth the name of Christ depart from iniquity."

Since there are two quotations here, the reader will need to make a substantial pause after the first quotation, and also a shorter pause after *And*.

Finally, Daniel 6:13:

> Then answered they and said before the king, That Daniel, which is of the children of the captivity of Judah, regardeth not thee, O king, nor the decree that thou hast signed, but maketh his petition three times a day.

A casual look at this verse might lead one to read this quotation as an indirect quotation: "They said . . . that Daniel . . . regardeth not thee . . . " But if you check with a modern translation, you will find that the word *that* is a demonstrative adjective, meaning that man Daniel. Therefore, since this is a direct quotation, beginning with *That Daniel*, (through to the end of the sentence) you need a pause after *the king*.

PRACTICE EXAMPLES

1. The speaker declared that, when Washington urged this country to steer clear of "entangling alliances," he was not advocating what we today call isolationism.

2. We having the same spirit of faith, according as it is written, I believed, and therefore have I spoken: we also believe, and therefore speak. (II Corinthians 4:13)

3. But go ye and learn what that meaneth, I will have mercy, and not sacrifice: for I am not come to call the righteous, but sinners to repentance. (Matthew 9:13)

4. And behold, I will send a lad, saying Go, find out the arrows. If I expressly say unto the lad, Behold, the arrows are on this side of thee, take them: then come thou: for there is peace to thee, and no hurt: (I Samuel 20:21)

DISCUSSION

1. If you pause before *entangling,* you make your listeners see quotation marks rather than your meaning. You could pause after *alliances.*

2. It is clear where the quotation begins here, after *written.* You might pause very slightly there. To make it clear where the quotation ends, you would need a pause after *spoken,* but not a falling inflection, as the verb of the whole sentence is still to come as *we also believe.*

3. You need to clarify for your listeners where Jesus is quoting, and where he is referring to himself. The quote is *I will have mercy and not sacrifice,* (Hosea 6:6), *I* in the quote refers to

God. You need a good pause after the quote, after *sacrifice,* to show that in the next phrase, Jesus is referring to himself—*I am not come to call the righteous. . . .* "

4. Putting in quotation marks is essential in this verse! The entire verse is dialogue, Jonathon talking to David. He tells David what he will be saying. There are 2 interior quotations: the first is '*Go, find out the arrows*'. You would need a slight pause after *lad,* and a good pause at the end of that quote. The next interior quotation is '*Behold, the arrows are on this side of thee, take them;*' You need a good pause after that quotation, to clarify that *take them* is what he will tell the lad, but the next phrase—*then come thou*—is what Jonathon is telling David to do.

35

Reading a Series

Sometimes a passage contains a series of things. You need to look at the list to see whether it is logical to break up the series into parts. Again, this is an application of the principle: What Does it Modify or Belong With.

Sometimes the first item in the series really is a general category, into which the remaining items fall.

> Lois brought with her a lot of clothes, four pairs of shoes, six dresses, five pantsuits, three sweaters, and twelve pairs of stockings.

The first item (clothes) is a general term, and the remaining items are the details. So it makes sense to make a longer pause after clothes (as if there were a colon there) and then to read the remaining items with shorter pauses after each.

Consider I John 2:16:

> For all that is in the world, the lust of the flesh, and the lust of the eyes, and the pride of life, is not of the Father, but is of the world.

Is this just a series of four things—or is the first (*all that is in the world*) a general category into which the other three things fit? If you believe that the first term is a general category, then you would make a longer pause after *world* and shorter pauses after *flesh, eyes, and life.*

Also this series in Isaiah 45:18:

> For thus saith the Lord that created the heavens; God himself that formed the earth and made it; he hath established it, he created it not in vain, he formed it to be inhabited: I am the Lord; and there is none else.

Here you should ask yourself, what is it that God did?

- He formed the earth and made it
- He established it
- He created it not in vain
- He formed it to be inhabited

You have here a series of four verbs followed by *it*. But the third has the negative *not* in it. That might be a clue that the last two in this series could be more closely linked—i.e., *not in vain* but *to be inhabited*. If you think that this analysis is sound, then you would pause after *made it* and after *established it*, but make only a very slight pause after *in vain*.

Look at Revelation 11:1:

> And there was given me a reed like unto a rod: and the angel stood, saying, Rise, and measure the temple of God, and the altar, and them that worship therein.

Here there is a series of three direct objects of the verb *measure*. The angel is directing the revelator to measure first, the temple, second, the altar, and third, the worshippers. The first two measurements could be physical. Do you think that the measurement of the worshippers is physical? Would the angel be directing the revelator to measure their height or their waistline? Probably not. If you agree, then wouldn't you want a longer pause after *altar*?

Consider I Kings 18:38. This is the story of the Lord accepting the sacrifice offered by Elijah, while the prophets of Baal looked on helplessly.

> Then the fire of the Lord fell, and consumed the burnt sacrifice, and the wood, and the stones, and the dust, and licked up the water that was in the trench.

How many things did *the fire of the Lord* consume? Five. Do any of these belong more closely together? Well, it's not too surprising, is it, that the fire consumed the burnt sacrifice and the wood? These are combustible. What about the stones and the dust? Isn't it more surprising that the fire would consume these? So perhaps these two could be put together. And, what is the most astonishing of all is that the fire actually *licked up the water in the trench.*

So to read this verse so as to bring out these various points, doesn't it make logical sense to use the following phrasing:

> Then the fire of the Lord fell, | and consumed the burnt sacrifice, and the wood, | and the stones, and the dust, | and | licked up the water that was in the trench.

While you should always look for ideas that belong more closely together, do not expect to find them in every series you come across. For example, when Paul lists the *works of the flesh* in Galatians 5:19-21, there isn't much that a reader can do except just plow through the list. You don't need to figure out a brilliant, new, surprising way to read passages like this one:

> [19] Now the works of the flesh are manifest, which are these; Adultery, fornication, uncleanness, lasciviousness, [20] Idolatry, witchcraft, hatred, variance, emulations, wrath, strife, seditions, heresies, [21] Envyings, murders, drunkenness, revellings, and such like:

PART SEVEN

Putting It All Together

36

Reading the Bible—Part One

The whole purpose of this chapter is to help you to read the Bible naturally and meaningfully. The King James Version of the Bible is one of the most difficult of books to read aloud, first, because it really **is** difficult due to its archaic language and constructions, and second because we **make** it difficult to read.

Reverence

Instead of letting their genuine reverence show itself naturally, many readers of the Bible may become over-awed, resulting in unpleasant straining and affectation. While it is important to be inspired to feel the spirit of the passage, technique is equally important. Good reading is combination of these two elements: inspiration and technique. Stressing the second and neglecting the first results in cold, colorless, uninspiring reading. An abundance of the first with none of the second lets your hearers know that you feel the spirit of the passage but fails to give them the meaning.

Colorless reading

The two main faults of Bible readers are (1) colorless reading, and (2) affected or overly dramatic reading. Although the latter is by far the more prevalent and objectionable, colorless reading, that is, reading with little variety or range, becomes monotonous and obscures the meaning. Frequently it is the result of not knowing how to phrase and emphasize. But this can be learned, as we have discussed in this book.

Dramatic or emotional reading.

Many otherwise good readers believe that as soon as they start to read the Bible they must dramatize and exaggerate their pronunciation and articulation. Let common sense and good taste be your guides. While you will need to speak a little more distinctly and more slowly, you want to avoid prolonging words so it doesn't come across like a chant. And don't act out words like *lift up, glorify, rejoice* or *triumph* by raising your pitch or your inflection—or your head. Once you feel sure of the meaning of a passage, read it as you would if it were not in the Bible. Try to forget the way you have heard a familiar and beautiful passage read all your life and examine it with fresh eyes.

Legitimate interpretation

Often, colorless reading results from a deliberate and well-meant attempt to avoid interpretation. Webster's New international Dictionary, Second Edition, defines the verb *to interpret* as:

> To apprehend and represent by means of art; to show by illustrative representation; as, an actor *interprets* a character; a musician, a sonata; an artist, a landscape.

This is what an oral reader is trying to do for his audience: Not personal interpretation but elucidation.

Unless you read everything in a dull and meaningless chant, you will be giving out some meaning or other. If you stress this word, you imply one meaning; if you stress that word, you imply something else.

Isn't it a good idea then, to settle upon the logical meaning of a passage and then study ways to phrase and emphasize in order to let this meaning come out, rather than to stumble along and sometimes unintentionally bring out meanings that neither you nor the author intend to convey?

We all use interpretation, whether we realize it or not; we are always deliberately pausing after one word and not after another, emphasizing one word and not another. See how phrasing makes all the difference in the meaning of Psalm 13:4:

> Lest mine enemy say | I have prevailed against him.

With the pause after *say* and before *I*, this indicates a quotation: My enemy is saying, "I have prevailed against him," meaning that he has prevailed against me. If it is read with no pause between *say* and *I*, it is made to mean exactly the opposite: that my enemy will say that **my** forces prevailed over him.

> Lest mine enemy say [that] **I** have prevailed against him.

The preceding verses in Psalms clearly indicate that the Psalmist is fearful that his enemy will prevail, so isn't the pause after *say* crucial in order to convey this meaning? Can this correct placing of a pause be called interpreting? If, in a conscientious attempt to avoid personal interpretation, you use no pauses at all, aren't you hiding the true meaning?

Consider Luke 2:43:

> And when they had fulfilled the days, as they returned, the child Jesus tarried behind in Jerusalem.

Did they fulfill the days as they returned? Or did Jesus tarry behind as they returned? If you make no pause after *days* and a long pause after *returned*, aren't you interpreting with the wrong meaning? But, if you pause long after *days* and only slightly if at all after *returned*, aren't you bringing out the logical meaning?

You may believe that your listeners will understand the meaning no matter how you phrase and emphasize, because everybody is familiar with the Bible. Some are; some aren't. Those who are will be distracted by illogical stress and pauses; those who aren't need to have it presented clearly. A clear presentation is needed especially in reading the less familiar verses.

Downright personal interpretation

There is such a thing, though, as really officious and blameworthy interpreting. Sometimes readers decide that they want a Bible passage to mean a certain thing and then give an outlandish twist to the phrasing or emphasis. This is downright personal interpretation and has nothing in common with the principles set forth in this book.

When words have different meanings

Often readers are puzzled over the exact meaning of some word or phrase in the King James Version, because English is not an exact language. In Revelation 4:11 you might not know whether *are* and *were created* are two different verbs (forms of *to be* and of *to create*) or merely two different tenses of the same verb, *to create.*

> For thou hast created all things, and for thy pleasure they are and were created.

If it is two tenses of *to create*, it means "for thy pleasure they are created and were created" and you would read it:

For thy pleasure they **are** and **were** |created.

You would stress *are* and *were*, since they are contrasts, and pause after *were*.

But if *are* is part of the verb *to be* instead of the verb *to create*, then the passage means "for thy pleasure they **exist** and were created," and you would slightly stress *are*, pause after *are*, subdue *were*, and stress *created*:

For thy pleasure they **are** | and were **created**.

Now which way will you read it? The two meanings are not the same. It means either one thing or the other. You can't avoid interpreting but are you going to bring out the right meaning? You don't want to guess, or decide what you **think** it should mean—that would be personally interpreting, and should be avoided. How can you make an intelligent choice with wording such as this?

Some students can turn to the Greek or Hebrew to determine which of the possible meanings is authentic. Many passages expressed in English will be ambiguous but their Greek renditions will be marvels of exactitude. However, those who don't know Hebrew or Greek can choose modern nondenominational translations to settle their questions. Here are some other translations of Revelation 4:11:

- Moffatt: . . . by thy will they existed and they were created.
- Revised Standard: . . . by thy will they existed and were created.
- New International: . . . by your will they were created and have their being.

Mannerisms

Much more annoying to most listeners than colorless reading is "fancy" reading or reading that has mannerisms. Many agree that they would rather listen to an untutored reader who makes honest mistakes than to a "trained" reader who reads affectedly or ornately. Mannerisms such as those below personalize the reading, causing the hearers to be conscious of the reader more than of the text, and are especially out of place in a reader of the Bible.

- ***The tendency to begin all sentences on a high pitch*** and then come down. In expressions like "O Lord" and "O God," used often in the Bible, some readers start with a high pitch on *O* and then drop on the second word. This makes it sound like a lament or an interjection rather than like a vocative, a word addressing the Lord, often in praise rather than in lamentation.

- ***Excessive sweetness.*** Approach your Bible-reading with reverence, of course, but avoid sounding melancholy, sanctimonious, or mournful. Also avoid a soothing tone. Many Bible readers give the impression they start each reading with: "Now, dear little children . . ."

- ***Affected joy.*** Don't try to put joy into your reading. If you feel the inspiration and joy in what you are reading, it will reveal itself naturally. But if you consciously try to inject joy, you are likely to sound false.

- ***Subduing all negative or unpleasant words.*** Some think these should be subdued and only affirmative or pleasant words should be emphasized. If you've gone this far in this book you know that frequently the negations are as important as the positive statements. If you always followed this policy of slighting negatives, in reading the twentieth chapter of Exodus you would suppress one of the most important passages in the Old Testament, since eight of the Ten Commandments are negative: Thou shalt not!

- ***Emphasizing every pronoun referring to God or to Jesus.*** Some feel that to fail to do this is irreverent. However, we don't do this in normal speech. To see what a peculiar effect such a practice brings about, read Matthew 8:23, emphasizing the pronouns that refer to Jesus:

  And when **he** was entered into a ship, **his** disciples followed **him**.

- ***Emphasizing too many words.*** Don't labor. Sometimes readers feel that every word in a Bible verse is so important, because of its sacred nature, that it must not be slighted. This produces the same effect as those who use no emphasis at all: utter colorlessness and meaninglessness. It is as if da Vinci had put no shadows or dark colors into his painting of *The Last Supper*. If everything had been painted bright, the figures of the people would have been indistinguishable from the background objects.

- ***Reading too slowly.*** Reading very slowly does not make one sound more reverent; nor does it make it easier for people to understand. It actually makes the reading harder to follow. The effective reader gives out a phrase rapidly and then pauses to let the hearer catch up. Thus, it takes him about the same amount of time to read a given passage as it does the one that reads the whole thing at a uniform rate of slowness with few noticeable pauses. It would be a very unsatisfactory symphony or concerto that performed very slowly over its whole composition, never rising to brighter and higher heights throughout the performance.

- ***Reading too fast.*** Most readers, especially beginners, read too fast. The best remedy for this is the same solution as for reading too slowly. Instead of trying to slow down on every word, decide on good places to pause and select several. Then be sure to pause at each of these places but not between them. Read each phrase fairly fast, if you like, but be sure to pause often.

Never underestimate your audience. Discriminating listeners are more numerous than most people think and are increasing in number. Even audiences that know little about grammar or technique appreciate clear reading. A person who knows nothing at all about cooking can tell whether a cake tastes good. A listener can usually figure out the meaning by a reader who does not know how to give the sense, just as a diner can add salt to the dish after it is cooked and served. But it is better to have it seasoned in advance.

37

Reading the Bible—Part Two

Miscellaneous special constructions

There are a number of special Biblical constructions which a reader should know how to handle. The translators of the King James Version often used the word *that* differently from the way we do today.

In Matthew 27:31 we find the expression *after that*, in a construction not usual today:

> And after that they had mocked him, they took the robe from off him.

Some readers stress the word *that* and pause before the first *they*, as though the word *that* were the object of the preposition *after*. However, *mocked him* is followed by a comma which shows that the main clause of the sentence is still to come. This type of construction is simple when you realize the word *that* in *after that* would be left out in modern English. All it means is *after.* Since you can't leave out the word *that* in your reading, you have to subdue it in such constructions. It means simply: and after they had mocked him.

Not every use of *after that* in the Bible means simply *after*. In John 11:7, *that* is really the object of *after* and the verse should be read with some stress on *that* and with a pause before *saith.*

> Then after **that** | saith he to his disciples, Let us go into Judaea again.

The King James Version uses *because that* where we would now say *because*. In Hebrews 10:2 we read:

> . . . because that the worshippers once purged should have had no more conscience of sins.

All we can do is to subdue the *that*.

II Corinthians 5:4 reads:

> For we that be in this tabernacle do groan, being burdened: not for that we would be unclothed, but clothed upon, that mortality might be swallowed up of life.

The expression *for that* would be, in modern English, *that* but we would not stress *that*. So we would read this verse with both *for* and *that* subdued.

Similarly *and* should be subdued in the expression *but and if* in Matthew 24:48:

> But and if that evil servant shall say in his heart...

If the passage you are reading contains unfamiliar words or words that are no longer a part of our language, as is often the case in Shakespeare or the Bible, substitute familiar words that mean the same thing and practice reading the passage with these substitutions. For instance, in the Bible the word *divers* means diverse, or different, and *severally* means separately. Practice reading verses like the following substituting the familiar word.

> But all these worketh that one and the selfsame Spirit, dividing to every man severally as he will. (I Corinthians 12:11)

> But all these worketh that one and the selfsame Spirit, dividing to every man separately as he will.

> Now when the sun was setting, all they that had any sick with divers diseases brought them unto him. (Luke 4:40)

Now when the sun was setting, all they that had any sick with different diseases brought them unto him.

Sometimes people stress *divers* instead of *diseases*, since *divers* looks strange and rather impressive. But if you remember that the phrase means different diseases, you will naturally stress *diseases* in this and every such passage. *Divers* is not pronounced like *diverse*, however. The accent is on the first syllable with a long "i".

In the instances where a direct quotation is preceded by the words "Verily, verily," readers often read these two words as a meaningless formula: verily-verily. But the actual meaning of the word *verily* is truly. You would pause slightly after the first *truly* and stress the second, as the reason for repeating it must have been for emphasis.

Verily, | **verily**, I say unto you, He that believeth on me, the works that I do shall he do also. (John 14:12)

The function of italics

Italicizing a word often indicates that the idea it carries is important and therefore the word should be emphasized. However, in the King James Version of the Bible an italicized word indicates that the word was supplied by the translators. Many of these italicized words are mere padding, inserted to smooth out the sentence. The latter part of Proverbs 27:10 reads: "*for* better *is* a neighbor *that is* near than a brother far off." If you omit the italicized words, the meaning is still perfectly clear.

Better a neighbor near than a brother far off.

Sometimes, realizing this, people come to the opposite conclusion that they can subdue every italicized word in the Bible. This policy is too simple. Although usually they are not important, there are instances where they are the crucial words in the sentence and need emphasis. In Exodus 4:7, Moses is told to put his leprous hand into his bosom and then pluck it out. The verse concludes with the statement that "It was turned again as his *other* flesh." You see that you could not omit *other* and still have the sentence make sense. Rather, you have to stress it, because *other* is a contrast with leprous flesh.

Italicized words in the King James Version may also indicate a word or words missing. For example, it is necessary to stress *given* in order to bring out the meaning in the following from John 7:39:

> But this spake he of the Spirit, which they that believe on him should receive: for the Holy Ghost was not yet *given*; because that Jesus was not yet glorified.

Consider the last phrase in John 8:6, which is entirely in italics:

> But Jesus stooped down, and with *his* finger wrote on the ground, *as though he heard them not*.

You could leave this phrase out, but doesn't it add a significant idea? Therefore wouldn't you stress either *heard* or *not?*

After Pilate tells Jesus that he had power to crucify or release him, Jesus answered:

> Thou couldest have no power *at all* against me, except it were given thee from above; (John 19:11)

Since Pilate has just mentioned the power that he has, you would probably stress *at all* in this verse.

In other books, the matter of italics presents other aspects to be considered. The three main functions are as follows:

The first function is the usual one: to indicate importance and therefore emphasis, as in:

> One witness said that at two o'clock he saw the defendant going *up* the *back* stairs; another, that he saw her going *down* the *front* stairs.

The second function is to set off a word which comes from a foreign language as in these three:

> Their boredom persisted, although they tried many diversions to offset this *ennui*.
>
> The whole place glowed with an atmosphere of *gemütlichkeit*.
>
> He insisted upon a writ of *habeas corpus*.

Whether such words are to be emphasized depends entirely on the sense of the sentence. When they do require stress, it is determined by the **meaning** and not by the italics. You would probably not emphasize *ennui* above, because it means the same as boredom in the same sentence. But you would stress it in this sentence:

> He enjoyed activities resulting from his many interests but his brother was burdened with persistent *ennui*.

Here, *ennui* would be emphasized, not because it is italicized but because it is in heavy contrast to *activities* and *interests*.

The third function of italics is to identify the word or phrase being discussed rather than employing its meaning in a sentence as in these two:

> On the final paragraph the word *separate* is misspelled.
>
> She didn't understand the term *oxymoron*.

You note that we italicize words in examples in this book to show which you would emphasize or subdue. Other devices such as quotation marks, underlining, and bold type, can be used to perform this third function of italics.

Pronunciation

Remember that the English language is fluid. Every day the pronunciations and usages in English are changing. Accepted usages become obsolescent and then obsolete. Scorned pronunciations gain approval. It is safer to say that a certain pronunciation is "accepted" or "not accepted" than to say it is "correct" or "incorrect." Both time and geography enter into the question. What is correct today may be incorrect tomorrow, and vice versa. What is correct here may be incorrect there, and vice versa.

A dictionary does not tell that you must use one pronunciation over any other. Instead the pronunciation listed by the dictionary means that at the present time this is the way the majority of educated speakers and readers pronounce that word. If there is more than one pronunciation given, they are equally acceptable.

The purpose of this section is to help you with certain words that are frequently mispronounced when read aloud. Rather than invoke diacritical marks to explain pronunciation, we will use rhymes. The pronunciations given here are from Webster's New International Dictionary, Second Edition, and are accepted usage today, particularly for words that are found in the King James Version of the Bible. When you are sure that you understand the pronunciations of these words, as illustrated by the rhymes, go to the dictionary and see how they are marked. Then this will help you in looking up other words. No attempt has been made to help you to overcome local speech patterns.

Most people have some, but these patterns are not within the province of this book.

Many experienced readers agree that it is the words you think you know how to pronounce that trip you. You will look up the long words that you are unfamiliar with. The little words are the ones that trick you.

One of the shortest words is one of the most often mispronounced: *and.* Almost everyone pronounces it correctly in conversation, but hand someone a script or a book and he is more than likely to give it an affected pronunciation.

Webster gives three pronunciations of *and.* If you stress it, you use a full short a, and it rhymes with *band,* not *wand.* You would use the stressed pronunciation in reading the second verse of the first chapter of Genesis: "And the earth was without form." However, using the stressed form every time the word *and* occurs would sound unnatural.

Webster lists also two unstressed forms, approximately *'nd* and *'n'.* The first unstressed pronunciation—'nd—can be appropriately used in formal as well as informal reading. You would use this pronunciation in Genesis 8:3, 7 " . . . after the end of the hundred 'nd fifty days the waters were abated." or " . . . he sent forth a raven, which went forth to 'nd fro. . . . "

The article *a* is usually pronounced like the first syllable of *above. A* is an obscure vowel, defined as an uncolored or weakened vowel. It is never pronounced like a long *a* (to rhyme with *bay)* unless there is a logical reason to stress it, as in saying, "Not a pack of wolves but just **a** wolf." Listen to newscasters using the long *a* and you can tell they are reading from the teleprompter.

An also is usually pronounced with an obscure vowel and sounds like the first syllable in *anew*. Only when it needs to be stressed is it pronounced with a short *a* (to rhyme with *ran*).

Not a bushel of apples, but **an** apple.

When the article *the* is placed before a word beginning with a consonant, the letter *e* has the obscure vowel sound, as in *agent.* It is almost un-pronounced, like *th'*, as in *th' banana.* But when *the* precedes a word beginning with a vowel, as in *the apple,* it is pronounced with the long *e*, as [thee] apple. The long *e* sound is also used when the word *the* is stressed, as in "not just any Mr. Shaw, but **the** [thee] Mr. Shaw."

The preposition *unto* is entirely obsolete and expresses nothing more than *to*. It is pronounced *unt" as in Luke 22:19,* "...and he gave unt' them." Though the accent falls on the first syllable the word does not get any stress at all. There's always something else around it that carries the meaning. If you substitute the word *to,* this is easy to see.

Biblical words often mispronounced

Saith has only one syllable. It means say-eth but is not pronounced that any more than *said* is pronounced say-ed. *Saith* should sound like *Seth.*

Shew is pronounced *show.*

Sloth rhymes with *both* or *broth.*

Err is a peculiar word, in that it rhymes with *blur* and has that sound of the vowel in all forms except *erring,* which has a choice of two vowel sounds. *Erring* may rhyme with either *blurring* or *herring.*

The first syllable of *comely* and of *compass* rhymes with *some.* They do not rhyme with either *comb* or *Tom.*

Sinew is sometimes mispronounced as *sin-oo* and *Matthew* as *Math-oo.* They should be *sin-yoo* and *Math-you.*

The first syllable of *ravening* rhymes with *have*. It does not rhyme with *brave*.

Resurrection is often given too fancy a pronunciation, with the second syllable pronounced as yoo. The first two syllables should be pronounced like the first two in *reservoir*.

Sometimes people try to pronounce *woman* just as it is spelled, to rhyme with *Roman*, but the first letters should sound like the first two letters in *wolf*, not in *woke*. And *women* rhymes with *swimmin'*.

Peniel has two permissible pronunciations. It may rhyme with *denial* or with *centennial*.

The first syllable of *authority* is *awe*, not *uh*, like the first syllable of *author*.

Zion starts with a z sound; *Sion*, with an s.

Rereward gives many a reader pause, as it looks like a form of the word *reward*. Rather, it is a variation of the word *rearward*, and means backward, to the rear, the opposite of *forward*. It has two syllables, and the first—*rere*—is pronounced just like *rear*.

Don't put extra letters into words. *Grievous* has only two syllables. There is no i after the v. It is *griev-us* (like *leave-us*), not *griev-i-us*, like *devious*.

There is no i after the v in *mischievous*. It is not *mis-cheev-i-us* (like *devious*). The first syllable is accented and the second is clipped instead of having an accented long e.

Throughly should not sound like *thoroughly*. It is pronounced as it is spelled, to rhyme with *truly*. *Thoroughly* is a different word.

Don't pronounce *height* as if it had an h after the t. Because of the th at the end of *length*, *depth*, *width*, and *breadth*, there is a tendency to add the same sound to *height*. Formerly *height* was spelled with an h at the end and was pronounced accordingly; but for a long time that spelling and pronunciation have not been considered good usage. *Height* rhymes with *kite.*

Sometimes even the letters that are actually there are not all to be pronounced. The *P* in Psalms should not be sounded. Neither should the *L*. *Psalms* rhymes with *palms.*

Terrestrial should be pronounced just as spelled. Because *celestial* is a word we use more often, people overlook the r after the second t in *terrestrial* and rhyme it with *celestial.* But *terrestrial* has four syllables, not just three. It is *te-res-tri-al,* not *ter-res-chul.*

Malefactor is sometimes given only three syllables, with a long *a* in the first: *male-fac-ter.* But it has four syllables and the first *a* is short: *mal-e*-fac-ter.

What about *blessed, cursed, hallowed, learned,* etc.? Webster gives two syllables for *blessed* [bless-ed], adding [the option] that it is "sometimes, as in verse, blest." *Cursed* may have two syllables or only one (*kurst*). *Hallowed* is two syllables but is often *hal-o-ed* in a liturgical style. *Learned*, as an adjective, may have one syllable or two.

Long *a* as in *ale* is used in *amen* but broad *a* as in *father* may be used and, in singing, must be used.

It may seem surprising to explain the pronunciation of *Jesus.* Surely it would seem that that would be a word everyone would know how to pronounce. Yes, but sometimes people are too careful in pronouncing it, using a full short *u* (as in *up*) in the second syllable, instead of an obscure vowel (as in *caucus*). It should be not *Jezuss* but *Jeez'ss.*

Do not scorn to apply the obscure vowel. They are one mark of an experienced speaker. The student or the inexperienced speaker or reader often strives to pro-nounce ev-e-ry let-ter in al-most a clock-work-man style. The professional speaker, comfortable with his diction is more likely to use obscure vowels , and therefore to sound more conversational. Webster gives the following examples of words with obscure vowels: a in ago, e in agent, I in sanity, o in comply, u in focus.

The *e* in *judgment* should be an obscure vowel, as in *silent*—when *silent* is pronounced naturally and spontaneously. As Webster's points out, the large majority of words with this obscure vowel *e* marking are pronounced with the obscure vowel sound, not with short *e* as in *end.* Short e should not be used in these words except, perhaps, when you are being extremely emphatic or when you are singing. It is *judgm'nt, commandm'nt, diffid'nt, Jerusal'm*—but not *Jerusalumm,* of course.

You don't need the short e sound to make the word clearly audible. No matter how large the auditorium in which you are reading, you don't need anything but the obscure vowel here. If you had to say "above the sofa" in Convention Hall, you would still pronounce both a's as obscure vowels. You wouldn't use short a's or long a's in order to be understood. You don't need to change your pronunciation to achieve audibility; change your articulation.

People often have a feeling that the pronunciation they don't use is better than the one they use. Before you change from one pronunciation to another, be sure that the one you adopt is authoritative. Usually the thing to work on is diction rather than changing from one accepted pronunciation to another. It is better to be plain and right than fancy and wrong.

38

Reading Poetry and Hymns

Many people are a little more hesitant about reading verse than about reading prose. Sometimes the meaning is not so easy to follow, because of inverted word order, for instance. Therefore, it is frequently advisable to rearrange verse into the normal prose order, then practice reading it in that form. See which words are emphasized and which are subdued and where you would pause. Then, when you read it again in its verse form, stress and subdue the same words and keep the same pauses even though the rhythm may call for different handling.

Due to the pronounced rhythm of some verse, there is a strong impulse to stop and punch the rhyme at the end of every line, whether the sense calls for a stop or not. Great familiarity with the material and how it's usually read, can lead us away from understanding, and therefore delivering, the real meaning. In the instance of a hymn or song, it must be phrased according to the stopping-places of the melody when sung. When you take the words away from the music and read them aloud, it is difficult to let go of the musical phrasing, even when it conflicts with the sense.

Another frequent mistake is wrong inflection, as in the following song lyrics by the Irish poet Thomas Moore.

Believe me, if all those endearing young charms,
Which I gaze on so fondly today,
Were to change by tomorrow and fleet in my arms,
Like fairy gifts fading away,
Thou would'st still be adored, as this moment thou art,
Let thy loveliness fade as it will,
And around the dear ruin each wish of my heart,
Would entwine itself verdantly still.

You might logically make a very slight pause after *charms* and after *arms*, because of the sense. But many people in reading the words aloud would not only pause after *charms* but stop, using a falling inflection as if it were the end of a sentence. Also, they would make no pause after *me*. The cause of such reading is easily found. It is the fact that the first eight words are the title of the song and usually are spoken in one gulp. If you think about the meaning you will read it in a fresher way: "Believe me: if all those endearing young charms were to change by tomorrow and fleet in my arms, thou would'st still be adored."

Sometimes a thought carries not only from one line over and back to the next but from one stanza to the next. If this is the case, do not pause at the end of a stanza any more than you would at the end of a line. Even when you are reading the words from a song book or a hymnal and one stanza ends at the bottom of the right-hand page and the next stanza begins at the top of the following left-hand page, if the thought carries over, don't hesitate a moment between stanzas. Remember: you are always trying to indicate to your hearers an idea rather than the arrangement of words on a page. Rhythm in singing poetry is more or less inflexible but rhythm in reading it should not be, unless one is interested solely in the musical effect and not in the significance.

Try reading aloud the first stanza of *America.*

My country, tis of thee,
Sweet land of liberty,
Of thee I sing.
Land where my fathers died!
Land of the Pilgrim's pride!
From every mountain side,
Let freedom ring!

You are an unusually discerning reader if you made a rather long pause before, and almost no pause after, *'tis of thee.* Because of the rhythm and the rhyme, most people read it just as they sing it, with no pause before *'tis of thee* and a long pause before *sweet land of liberty.* They read it as if My-country-'tis-of-thee were all one word. This phrasing is so habitual that the song is often called *My Country, 'Tis of Thee* instead of *America.* Yet those five words strung together make no sense without the eight that follow to complete the sentence.

You are talking to *My country* or *sweet land of liberty.* Therefore, they are both vocatives; so *sweet land of liberty* would naturally follow *'tis of thee* without a pause. *My country,* however, has nothing preceding it and you could read it naturally without a pause following it. However, since the line is most often heard without the pause before *'tis of thee*, it might be a good idea to pause noticeably between *country* and *'tis.*

Let's make up a sentence with exactly the same construction. Since this sentence is new to you, you will be more likely to approach it with a fresh eye:

My friend, it is of you, dear soul-mate, of you I am thinking.

The vocatives, *my friend,* and *dear soul-mate,* correspond to *My country* and *Sweet land of liberty,* respectively; *it is of you* corresponds with *'tis of thee,* and *of you I am thinking* corresponds with *of thee I sing.* Now you may or may not pause after *friend;* you probably will pause after *dear soul-mate;* but, if you read it as you would speak it, you will certainly not pause before *dear soul-mate.* And you probably would pause between *soul-mate* and *of you I am thinking:*

My friend,| it is of you,_dear soul-mate,| of you I am thinking.

There is exactly the same construction in the fourth stanza:

Our fathers' God to Thee,
Author of Liberty,
To Thee we sing,

It is usually read the way it has to be sung, as:

Our-fathers'-God-to-Thee, | Author of Liberty to Thee we sing.

But read aloud, it should be:

Our fathers' God, | to Thee, (Author of Liberty),| To Thee we sing.

39

Inflection

As briefly explained in Chapter 3, inflection is changing pitch within a syllable. The word *inflection* comes from a Latin word meaning *to bend.* Hence, it is a bending of the voice. The three primary kinds of inflection are rising, falling and circumflex. To review:

Rising [↑] inflection is one in which the voice begins a syllable on one pitch and then rises to a higher one. Rising inflections are used to denote doubt, uncertainty, suspense, confusion and suggest an incomplete thought or lack of finality. However, a rising inflection is also used on a direct question that expects an answer of *yes* or *no*, as in "Are you going to the party?" ↑

Falling [↓] inflection is just the opposite: the voice begins a syllable on one pitch and then falls to a lower one. Falling inflections end most sentences and denote finality, strength and complete thoughts. They also end interrogative questions or those which require more than a *yes/no* answer. "How are you getting there?" ↓

Circumflex [⤻] inflection is a bending around using both rising and falling inflections. Although there are two types of circumflex (rising and falling) we use the rising form most often in our conversation. A falling circumflex (down-up-down - ↷) is often used to denote something insinuating, untrustworthy or indicates uncertainty, sarcasm, evasion.

A rising circumflex is the opposite. It starts on a higher tone, the pitch lowers and then comes back up (up-down-up - ↶). It's used on the vowel in the last syllable of a word, whether or not that word is stressed. There's a great deal of rising circumflex in our voices when we talk, especially at the ends of phrases. They indicate to the listener that although we may be taking a pause, we haven't finished speaking or reading. It's also used to indicate the first element of a contrast (It's not **red**, ↶ it's **green**. ↓) and for a variety of other reasons. Unfortunately, it's a vocal aspect that's often eliminated when reading prepared material such as the Bible.

Sometimes people include a fourth type of inflection—level or straight. However, it isn't really an inflection at all, because there's no change of pitch. When there's no pitch change the result is a monotone. Generally, we want to avoid that.

Inflections are the melody of our speech. They add interest and expression to what we say. Sometimes when we read they are either eliminated and the delivery becomes flat, or the reader uses so many of them that the listener becomes more aware of **how** something is read rather than focusing on **what** is read.

Questions

The use of rising inflections on *Yes/No* type questions and of falling inflections on all other questions is not an inflexible rule. One exception is when a non-Yes/No question is followed immediately by the answer from the same source. In this case, a rising inflection might be the better choice.

For example, in Psalm 24:

> [9] Lift up your heads, O ye gates; even lift them up, ye everlasting doors; and the King of glory shall come in. [10] Who is this King of glory? ↑ The LORD of hosts, he is the King of glory. ↓

In the question, *King of glory* is clearly an old idea, and the logical stress would fall on the verb *is.* At the end of the question you would use a rising inflection.

Mutually exclusive questions

Sometimes we encounter a series of questions, all of which can be answered by *Yes* or *No*, but where a *Yes* answer to one question will require a *No* answer to another question. We call such a series mutually exclusive questions.

One of the most obvious examples in the Bible is in Luke 7:20:

> When the men were come unto him, they said, John Baptist hath sent us unto thee, saying, Art thou he that should come? Or look we for another?

Both questions in the verse can be answered by "Yes" or "No." But clearly, if one answers "Yes" to the first question, "No" must be the answer to the second. Therefore, the logical inflections to use are a rising inflection on the first and a falling on the second.

Completely falling inflection

The completely falling inflection comes at the end of an idea, although it may not necessarily come at the end of the sentence. It denotes finality. In complicated sentences, avoid a completely falling inflection until after the main verb and its object (if any).

Consider Acts 8:

> [27] Behold, a man of Ethiopia, an eunuch of great authority under Candace queen of the Ethiopians, who had the charge of all her treasure, and had come to Jerusalem for to worship, [28] was returning, and sitting in his chariot read Esaias the prophet.

First, look for the subject: *man of Ethiopia*. Then, find the main verb. (In this case, there are two: *was returning* and *read*.) It would be possible to use a completely falling inflection on *returning*, since that is one of the main verbs. However, the reader could also use a partially falling inflection and not use a completely falling inflection until the end of the sentence on the word *prophet*.

More on the circumflex inflection

Using the same verse, let's look at how the circumflex can be used to keep a sentence moving forward, especially when it's very long. In conversation, we'll often use a circumflex:

- to indicate that, although we may be pausing for breath or meaning, we haven't finished our thought.
- at the beginning and end of parenthetical expressions.
- on the first element of a contrast or comparison.

Isn't the phase, *an eunuch of great authority under Candace queen of the Ethiopians, who had the charge of all her treasure, and had come to Jerusalem for to worship*, parenthetical? Since in conversation we pause and circumflex around a parenthetical expression, wouldn't you do so at *Ethiopia* and *worship*?

> [27] Behold, a man of Ethiopia ⤻, / an eunuch of great authority under Candace queen of the Ethiopians, who had the charge of all her treasure, and had come to Jerusalem for to worship

> ↺, / [28] was returning, and sitting in his chariot read Esaias the prophet.

Now, let's look at the other phrases. Since the idea is not complete at those points and to keep the verse moving, there would also be circumflexes in those places.

> [27] Behold, a man of Ethiopia ↺, / an eunuch of great authority under Candace queen of the Ethiopians ↺ , who had the charge of all her treasure ↺, and had come to Jerusalem for to worship ↺, / [28] was returning ↓ , and sitting in his chariot ↺, read Esaias the prophet ↓.

Because Analogies and Common Denominators contain comparisons and contrasts, circumflex inflections are used on the first part of each. We do this naturally and spontaneously in conversation, and should do the same in reading.

Deuteronomy 8:5 reads:

> As a man chasteneth his son, so the Lord thy God chasteneth thee.

As we have seen, we subdue the common denominator *chasteneth* both times and emphasize *man* and *God* as the first contrast and *son* and *thee* as the second contrast. And we use a circumflex inflection on *man*, *son* and *God* and a completely falling inflection on *thee*.

> As a **man** ↺ chasteneth his **son** ↺, so the Lord thy **God** ↺ chasteneth **thee** ↓.

Degrees of inflection

Not all inflections consistently use the same pitches; some are higher and some lower. How you modify them depends on what you're saying or reading. A falling inflection might drop just a couple of notes in the middle of a sentence, but then fall much lower at the end of the sentence. A series of circumflexes, such as we had in Acts 8, would also have a variety of pitch changes. If they're all the same, the reading can become patterned and boring. To experience the variety of inflectional sounds, try these:

- Say the word *Oh* using 3 different levels of falling pitch. Oh. Oh! Oh!!
- Do the same with rising. Oh? Oh?? Oh???
- Finally, with a rising circumflex. Oh? Oh?? Oh???

The distinctions between rising and rising circumflex might be hard to hear. Just remember that a rising pitch ends up (down-up ↑) but a rising circumflex starts up, comes back down, and then ends up (up-down-up ⤻). It might feel and sound like a loop in the voice.

Some readers have a mannerism of using too many falling inflections. This produces a choppy, disconnected effect. Try reading Matthew 14:15 with completely falling inflections on *evening, him, saying, place, past, away, villages* and *victuals.*

> And when it was *evening* ↓ , his disciples came to *him* ↓ , *saying* ↓ , This is a desert *place* ↓ , and the time is now *past* ↓ ; send the multitude *away* ↓ , that they may go into the *villages* ↓ , and buy themselves *victuals* ↓ .

Didn't that produce an unnatural and strangely rhythmic reading? Now try replacing some of those falling inflections with rising and circumflex inflections. Notice how it more connected and conversational it sounds.

And when it was evening ↺ , his disciples came to him ↓ , saying ↺ , This is a desert place ↓ or ↺ , and the time is now past; ↓ send the multitude away ↺ , that they may go into the villages ↺ or ↓ and buy themselves victuals ↓ .

When we read to children, we use a great deal of inflection to add interest and excitement. However, if we read the same way to an adult audience, it can sound theatrical, put on and as if we're talking down to them. Remember, we don't want the listener to become so aware of how something is read, that they don't hear what is read.

The subject of inflections is highly complex, and this book can illustrate only a few examples of their use. The important thing for a reader is to understand a passage thoroughly and then to think through the implications of the inflections being used.

PRACTICE EXAMPLES

1. So the servants of the householder came and said unto him, Sir, didst not thou sow good seed in thy field? from whence then hath it tares? (Matthew 13:27)
2. Where is the wise? Where is the scribe? Where is the disputer of this world? Hath not God made foolish the wisdom of this world? (I Corinthians 1: 20)
3. Who shall separate us from the love of Christ? Shall tribulation, or distress, or persecution, or famine, or nakedness, or peril, or sword? (Romans 8: 35)
4. And he said, Who told thee that thou wast naked? Hast thou eaten of the tree, whereof I commanded thee that thou shouldest not eat? (Genesis 3: 11)

DISCUSSION

1. Rising inflection on the first question; falling on the second.
2. Falling inflection on the first three questions, rising on the fourth.
3. Falling inflection on the first question, rising on the second.
4. Falling inflection on the first question, rising on the second.

40

Platform Manner

The techniques and principles stated in this book provide a clear and practical method for any reader to not only find the author's meaning in their text but to then clearly and conversationally express that meaning when reading aloud. In addition, effective delivery of these techniques and principles requires consideration of the many elements of presentation such as, preparation, physical setting, projection, use of a sound system, appropriate demeanor and attire, as well as presence and spontaneity.

It is has been proven that even great content is not able to save a bad presentation.

Preparation

Preparation allows the message to be presented seamlessly. The mechanics of presenting before an audience should be well planned and rehearsed to minimize distractions during the reading. Make sure that your passages are properly marked and tabulated and that your materials are placed appropriately for easy access and transition. Be thoroughly familiar with your readings, including pronunciations, and practice reading them aloud more than once before you present. If necessary, write down the order of your presentation and keep it visible.

Make sure you have a clear sense of sequence and transitions, if there are any. Be prepared to turn a page in the middle of a sentence by putting your finger under the next page before you have to turn it. Nothing sounds much more amateurish than to stop in the middle of a sentence while you struggle to find a place.

Consider getting yourself a mini recorder and talk to it—in your car, kitchen or anywhere else. Describe a movie, tell a joke or read some of your text. Play it back and see how it sounds. Spend some time with your voice—others do.

Physical setting

Become familiar with the physical setting in which you will present. Note the size of the room, the acoustics, the distance between your position and the audience. Become comfortable with using the furniture on the platform. Practice entering and exiting, walking to the podium, sitting, getting up and standing. Adjust the height of the desk if necessary, and make sure the lighting is effective, not casting shadows. Test and adjust the sound system if using one. Also check to see if there is any distracting sound from ventilating or heating systems that may need to be dealt with, either to be turned off or to adjust the mikes to compensate.

No one comes to hear a reading with the expectation of failure.

The desk has one reason for being there, and that is to hold up the reader's text. Its principal disadvantage is that it forms a barrier between reader and audience. There are a couple of ways to overcome this barrier. First, don't let your text pull your attention down. Beware of reading "into the book" by tilting your head down toward the desk. With some practice your head can be slightly angled up while your eyes are still focused on the text. This small adjustment makes a tremendous difference in including your audience.

Eye contact

Some people are uncomfortable when a reader of the Bible makes eye contact with them. It breaks the connection with the message and puts it on the messenger. "Does the reader mean to imply what he just read is about me?" You can focus on the back of the room when you look up from the reading, but not always at the same spot. Some of these opportunities may occur in transition moments or in the beginning or ending of a presentation. "Cocktail party eyes"—over, around and through but never at, reads self-consciousness. It's fine to look directly at individuals for a second or two and then, move on.

When you find you are sharing a space and it comes time for the other person to read or speak, completely yield your attention to that person. Keeping your eyes either down or in the general direction of the speaker does the trick. Looking up into a corner or out a window is very distracting and leaves the audience wondering what, over there, is so thoroughly grabbing your attention.

When reading announcements or your own material, eye contact at appropriate intervals can connect you with your listeners.

Gestures

Some people can't speak without gesturing. It's a natural form of expression. Even radio announcers sometimes gesture before the microphone. When you are reading, however, it is not about you, but the writer. It's best to keep your arms and hands to yourself. Besides, you need your hands to manage the pages of the book or other document.

You also do not want to emphasize with your head. Some readers seem unable to stress a word vocally without also jerking their heads downwards. This is a habit well worth overcoming, because it annoys your audience and focuses attention on you instead of on what you are reading. Most people who do this aren't aware of it. Ask a friend to watch you read; or practice selections from memory in front of a mirror.

A third form of gesturing is your facial expression. Be natural, unself-conscious. Let the meaning of what you are reading form your expression naturally. Be careful not to force this. Audiences can tell a put-on facial expression and it disconnects them from the reading. If what you are reading is joyous, you will be surprised how a smile affects your tone and connects the words with the audience. When you read something serious, naturally you would not smile. Your expression should change to whatever you are feeling about that passage as long as you are thinking about the passage and not your expression. If you are always solemn, you must not be thinking about what you are reading. Even an obituary has its high moments.

In addition to head bobbing and eye roving, beware of other mannerisms that can detract from your reading like raising and lowering your eyebrows, standing with one shoulder higher than the other, or fiddling with a pencil or jewelry, etc. Since the person who does these things is almost unconscious of them, it is a good idea to ask a friend if you are forming any of these habits.

Clothing

Wear clothing that is respectful of the audience and not distracting. Know your audience and what they expect of a presenter.

Wear clothing that is comfortable, that allows you to move easily on the platform, to sit and stand without twisting or stressing the fabric. And once on the platform you don't want to have to fuss with your clothing or any accessories. If in doubt, it is always good to have a "dress" rehearsal. As for accessories, leave home any jewelry that might flash in the light. Do not wear a wristwatch or bracelet that clinks when you move your wrist.

Volume

Finally, none of what we have discussed will matter if you can't be heard—all the way to the back of the room. When you speak extemporarily to a group, your focus is on the audience, and your voice adjusts naturally to reach those you are talking to. It's similar to naturally adjusting the focus of your eyes to see things at different distances. But when one is reading from a text, the temptation is to focus on the text, or at most those in the first row, and those at the back of the room have to strain to hear. If you are more conscious of the volume of the room than the volume of your voice, you will be heard.

If your podium has amplification, this is not license to mumble into the microphone. The purpose of amplification is not to make your voice louder, but clearer; and to fill all the "dead" spots in the room. Though you certainly need to have the microphone correctly positioned, you still need to speak out as if there were no amplification. You still must project in order to be heard clearly.

Presence

When you rise and walk forward, approach your audience, not the desk. It's a subtle difference but by keeping your focus up and out you will be signaling a welcome without saying a word. After you rise, wait a moment before you begin to talk or read. Greet them with a smile, fresh and inviting. Be sure that your hearers are calm and receptive before you begin. (Some speakers call this "subduing your audience.") You can use these moments for some quiet deep breathing also.

If there is a technical malfunction or you are momentarily distracted by something that disturbs your focus, the best action is to take a moment to adjust, get back on track and then continue on with grace. No need to comment or apologize. This puts the audience at ease and reconnects them with the reading. If a fly lights on your face the least distracting move is to brush it off. You don't want a fly to upstage the reading.

Know that your audience is receptive or they wouldn't be there. Remember that no one comes to hear someone present with the expectation of failure.

41

Working with Coaches

We hope that by the time you have finished the basics of emphasis and of phrasing, you have gained a good idea of what conversational reading is, and after getting into some of the additional principles of emphasis and phrasing you feel confident that you can give your listeners the sense of what the writer intended. So what is next?

Many students of this book will find it easier to apply these principles by having someone experienced in the use of these speech patterns hear you read. It takes a practiced ear to hear oneself; therefore enlisting an independent set of ears is helpful. You may have intended to emphasize a certain word but not realized you had also emphasized other words you did not want to stress. Or you might not have emphasized the word clearly enough for the listener to get it. We know we need to subdue certain words—sometimes whole strings of words—but as we said earlier, subduing is hard for a lot of readers. A good coach will catch these.

Beware of the coach who tells you **how** to read a passage, or worse, reads it so you can parrot his reading. You as the reader must determine what the message is that you will read. Those who selected you, want you to read it in your own voice, not in your coach's voice. Attempting to dictate to people how to read a document would be presumptuous—and in the case of the Bible almost sacrilegious.

Coaches authorized by the Institute of Analytical Reading, the publisher of this book, teach by asking the questions that can draw your attention to opportunities to bring out a larger sense of the material and help you discover the writer's meaning yourself. Your answers to these questions will lead you to see a carry-over or common denominator you might have missed. At no time during coaching sessions by any member of the Institute of Analytical Reading will readers be told what a passage or citation or compilation means.

It takes a practiced ear to hear oneself.

Coaching can be done in person, through face-to-face technology like Skype, or over the telephone. If the student reader is familiar with the principles in this book, after a few one hour introductory sessions, the student and coach can start working with material the student is tasked to read before a group. If the student is not yet comfortable with the principles in this book, he or she might want to attend one of the Institute's classes on the basics.

CONCLUSION

All the ideas offered in this handbook are given in order to help you do two things: to give out the writer's real meaning; and to sound natural and conversational.

Skimming this book will not make you a good reader any more than skimming a Beethoven score would make you a good conductor. Make these principles your servants. Don't serve them. Always let common sense be your final test. Remember that reading well is not just a science but an art supported by a scientific technique.

Giving the Sense is about understanding what you are reading and then sharing that understanding of the writer's meaning with your listeners. We hope you can put the principles in this handbook into practice and that they help you, as they have helped all our students, excel at giving the sense. You can do this, and what a gift it will be for your listeners.

And all the people went their way . . .
to make great mirth
because they understood the words that
were declared unto them.

NEHEMIAH 8:12

The Institute of Analytical Reading

The Institute of Analytical Reading is an affiliation of experienced readers who have completed an intensive two week course of 120 hours in the teaching and coaching of conversational principles. Having each already used these principles in their own experience as a reader of the written word, they are taught in this course how to teach others these principles, and how to coach students in their use of Analytical Reading.

Analytical Reading instructors teach by the Socratic method. Questions from the teacher help the students analyze passages for themselves. Students are not told how they must read a passage.

Students learn to apply the pertinent principle and then decide for themselves how to read the passage. The question and answer technique is used in a conscientious effort to avoid influencing the pupil's thinking and to guard against imitating the teacher.

Approved teachers of Analytical Reading are listed in the Institute's website. Only teachers who have completed the Institute's teacher's training and have pledged to uphold the Institute's standards can be listed. Since the majority of the teaching is done by phone or Skype, location isn't a major factor in deciding who to call from the list of affiliates. Most teachers will also travel when necessary to teach a class at your location.

ISBN 978-194517024-9

CPSIA information can be obtained
at www.ICGtesting.com
Printed in the USA
LVOW04*1024141016
508760LV00003B/5/P